Danger (

Dagenham

Danger Over Dagenham

Prepared and compiled by
John Gerard O'Leary

Prepared for publication by Derek Alexander

VALENCE HOUSE
a place of discovery

Valence House Publications

Published in 2018 by Valence House Publications
Valence House, Becontree Avenue
Dagenham, Essex RM8 3HT

www.valencehousecollections.co.uk

ISBN 978-1-911391-06-7

Previous Publications
Abyssinia 1868 Last Great Expedition of Queen Victoria's
Army (978-1-911391-02-9)
Sebastopol to Dagenham (978-1-911391-02-9)
A History of Dagenham (978-1-911391-03-6)
The Life of Sir Richard Fanshawe (978-1-911391-00-5)
The Death of the 'Dukes' (978-1-911391-99-9)

Cover Images :
Bomb Damage at Peartree Gardens, Dagenham 1939 - 1945
LBBD Archives at Valence House

Biography of J. G. O'Leary

John Gerard O'Leary came to Dagenham in 1929 at the age of 29 having previously worked in libraries in Kensington, Fulham, St. Pancras and Bethnal Green.

When Dagenham became an Urban District in 1926 it applied for powers to provide a library service and these were granted in 1928. John O'Leary saw his task as starting "a new library service on £2,000, enormous hope and enthusiasm!" In the early years of the service temporary libraries were opened and existing buildings were adapted, until in 1934 the first purpose built library, Rectory library, was opened. Every opportunity was taken to develop and improve the library service through John O'Leary's pioneering spirit.

The service that John O'Leary established was unique in that the concept of a truly free library service was realised as no fines or reservation charges were made. He initiated an imaginative publications programme and wrote the 'Book of Dagenham' and 'Dagenham Place Names', as well as finding time to edit the 'Dagenham Digest', the 'Essex Review', the 'Essex Journal' and the 'Essex Recusant', for varying periods. Among the other offices he held were those of Secretary of the Victoria Council History of Essex and Secretary of the Dagenham Arts Council.

He had a passionate interest in local history research, building up the Museum collection at Valence House and organising impressive exhibitions on local history themes. His work in this field was recognised by his election as a Fellow of the Society of Antiquaries.

It is for his service as Borough Librarian of Dagenham from 1929 to 1965, in establishing and developing the library service, and for his valuable work in the field of local history the Museum Room at Valence House was renamed the John Gerard O'Leary room in his memory.

Exhibitions : The Essex of Chaucer May 1954

Introductory talk to school children by the Borough Librarian

LBBD Archives at Valence House (EES1646)

Exhibitions : The Essex of Chaucer May 1954

School children being conducted round the exhibition by the Borough Librarian

LBBD Archives at Valence House (EES1644)

DANGER OVER
DAGENHAM
1939-45

BOROUGH OF DAGENHAM
MAY, 1947

Borough of Dagenham Bomb Map

LBBD Archives at Valence House (BD1/K/1)

Please come and see a much larger version of the map at the archives

BOROUGH OF DAGENHAM

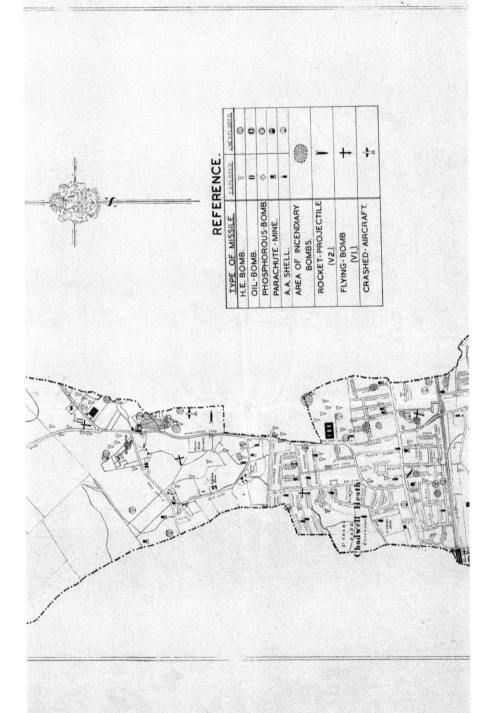

REFERENCE.

TYPE OF MISSILE.	EXPLODED	UNEXPLODED
H.E. BOMB.	▽	⊕
OIL-BOMB.	▥	⬚
PHOSPHOROUS-BOMB.	◇	◉
PARACHUTE-MINE.	▦	◉
A.A. SHELL.	▦	⊕
AREA OF INCENDIARY BOMBS.		●
ROCKET-PROJECTILE (V2.)		╂
FLYING-BOMB (V1.)		✝
CRASHED-AIRCRAFT.		✈

Chadwell Heath

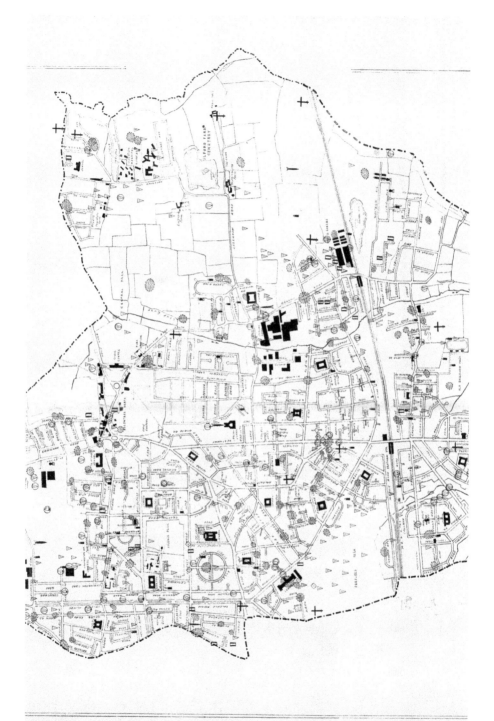

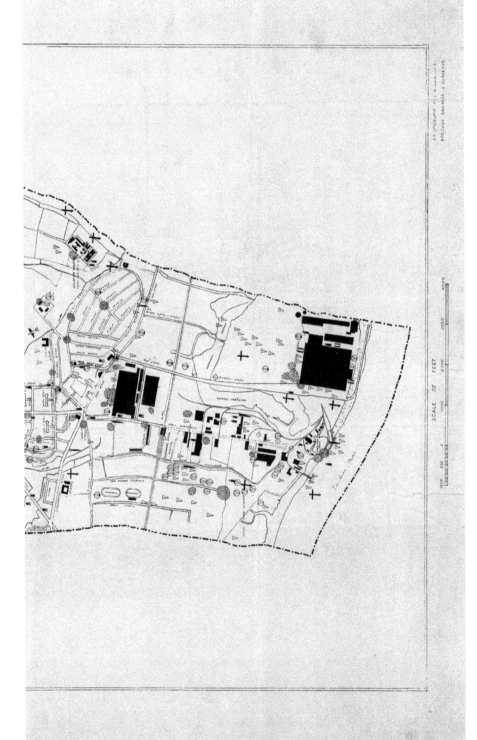

SCALE OF FEET

CONTENTS

FOREWORD

THIS book is a bare record of fact, of work achieved under conditions never before experienced in the history of the world. It is the story of the men and women of Dagenham who, midst all these new stresses and strains, carried on with the business of everyday life—everyday war life.

Except for a very brief period in 1939, after the first evacuation, the schools never closed. Every common requirement of everyday life continued—the dustman, the postman, the paper boy and the milkman never missed their customary rounds, although the night had been a holocaust of noise. The carts and vans went up to the markets and the work of the nearby farms continued its unaltering pace. The trains, buses and trams continued on their respective ways.

It is not without significance that this book is almost devoid of individual names (apart from those who died) because it is meant to be a tribute to the whole of the people of Dagenham. It is a tribute to Civil Defence workers and to the men and women in the factories, as well as the mothers of families (particularly those) who were sometimes away with the children in the country grieving over the fate of their homes and husbands here.

During the " year of Munich," before public consciousness was aware of Civil Defence, the machinery was put in motion. The war-time duties of the permanent officials were drawn up. The Controller for Civil Defence, Mr. F. C. Lloyd (Borough Engineer), died suddenly in the midst of the war (a death perhaps accelerated by his duties), and was succeeded by Mr. A. F. Stickland. The First Aid and Casualty Services came under Dr. C. Herington (Medical Officer of Health), Food Control, Emergency Feeding and British Restaurants were under Mr. H. O. Bigg (Borough Treasurer), a number of miscellaneous duties (such as care of personal effects and the Information Service) were the responsibility of the Town Clerk (Mr. F. W. Allen) or officers of his department. The duties of Evacuation Officer and Fuel Overseer were carried out by Mr. John O'Leary (Borough Librarian), a task in which he placed human considerations before Government regulations on many occasions. The head of each service had a good team of deputies and staff who responded well to extra and new duties.

The Members of the Council (their names are found on a preceding page) carried their share of the burden in Committee, in Council and in endless inspections and visitations. One lost his life on duty fire watching —Alderman W. F. Legon. All the normal social and essential services were maintained side-by-side with the war services, and attendance to Council and Committee business went on uninterrupted, although the noise overhead often seemed strangely at variance with the matters under discussion.

The Emergency Committee consisted of Aldermen Chorley, Clack, Mrs. Evans and F. Brown. This Committee carried the weight of all Civil Defence Committees concerned not only with public safety but with succour and comfort.

Few, very few, names have been mentioned because this record belongs to all people who lived up to the motto of the Borough—" Judge us by our deeds."

ANON.

ROLL OF HONOUR

OF THOSE KILLED BY ENEMY ACTION

Name	Address	Age	Date of Death
Onslow, H.	122, Chittys Lane	35	15/ 9/40
Reeves, W. R.	183, Eton Road, Ilford	37	18/ 9/40
Bailey, Ernest	2, Freshwater Road	14	19/ 9/40
Bailey, Mrs. Dorothy	2, Freshwater Road	38	19/ 9/40
Bailey, William	2, Freshwater Road	43	19/ 9/40
Duke, George	48, Surrey Road	7	20/ 9/40
Duke, David	48, Surrey Road	2	20/ 9/40
Hoy, Miss Kitty	7, Cartwright Road	23	21/ 9/40
Ellingworth, C.P.O.	362, Copner Road, Portsmouth	—	21/ 9/40
Ryan, Lt.-Comdr. R. H.	Gosport	—	21/ 9/40
Duke, Mrs. Lilian	48, Surrey Road	30	22/ 9/40
Lennox, Kenneth	31, Gordon Road, Chadwell Hth.	10	22/ 9/40
Lennox, Mr. Sidney	31, Gordon Road, Chadwell Hth.	45	22/ 9/40
Lennox, Mrs. Elizabeth	31, Gordon Road, Chadwell Hth.	35	22/ 9/40
Lennox, Ronald Victor	31, Gordon Road, Chadwell Hth.	4	23/ 9/40
Evans, Charles	29, Ford Road	33	23/ 9/40
Evans, Emma	29, Ford Road	35	23/ 9/40
Evans, Joyce	29, Ford Road	12	23/ 9/40
Evans, Raymond	29, Ford Road	9	23/ 9/40
Evans, Bryan	29, Ford Road	2	23/ 9/40
Mollenhoff, Ernest	219, Hunters Square	29	30/ 9/40
Mollenhoff, Ethel	219, Hunters Square	28	30/ 9/40
Hopkins, Rosina	145, Grafton Road	24	30/ 9/40
Hopkins, Harry	145, Grafton Road	26	30/ 9/40
Neall, James	59, Oglethorpe Road	34	2/10/40
Neall, Charlotte	59, Oglethorpe Road	33	2/10/40
Brown, Dennis	230, Halbutt Street	30	5/10/40
Brown, Moira	230, Halbutt Street	6	5/10/40
Cole, Mary	3, Halbutt Gardens	7	5/10/40
Macey, John H.	3, Halbutt Gardens	26	5/10/40
Cole, Mrs.	3, Halbutt Gardens	—	5/10/40
Cole, Thomas	3, Halbutt Gardens	12	5/10/40
Roberts, Eunice	234, Halbutt Street	—	5/10/40
Lamb, Mr.	46, Windsor Road	75	5/10/40
Lamb, Mrs.	46, Windsor Road	69	5/10/40
Mann, Mrs. Florence	232, Halbutt Street	29	5/10/40
Mann, John	232, Halbutt Street	34	5/10/40
Mann, Mrs. Elizabeth	232, Halbutt Street	34	5/10/40
Mann, Charles	232, Halbutt Street	6	5/10/40
Mann, Iris	232, Halbutt Street	4	5/10/40
Mann, Joyce	232, Halbutt Street	1	5/10/40
Mann, Mr. George	232, Halbutt Street	28	5/10/40
Mann, Mr. James	232, Halbutt Street	—	5/10/40
Mann, Mrs. Eliz. (Snr.)	232, Halbutt Street	—	5/10/40
Mann, Anne	232, Halbutt Street	32	5/10/40
Mann, Lilian	232, Halbutt Street	30	5/10/40
Martin, Elizabeth	52, Windsor Road	24	5/10/40
Martin, Henry	52, Windsor Road	35	5/10/40
Martin, Ronald	52, Windsor Road	3 mths.	5/10/40
Martin, Sylvia	52, Windsor Road	3	5/10/40
Ash, Lt. (Bomb Dis. Sqd.)	Barracks, Gordon Fields, Ilford	—	7/10/40
Foster, Lt. (B.D.S.)	Barracks, Gordon Fields, Ilford	—	7/10/40
Lewis, Sapper	Barracks, Gordon Fields, Ilford	—	7/10/40
Websdale, Sapper	Barracks, Gordon Fields, Ilford	—	7/10/40
Hitchcock, Sapper	Barracks, Gordon Fields, Ilford	—	7/10/40

Name	Address	Age	Date of Death
Kelly, Denis G.	85, Sisley Road, Barking	35	15/10/40
Dorrington, Mrs. M.	10, Vicarage Road	63	15/10/40
Race, Pauline	14, Vicarage Road	2	15/10/40
Race, Frederick	14, Vicarage Road	3	15/10/40
Race, Peggy	14, Vicarage Road	12	15/10/40
Alcock, L.A.C.	169, Ballards Road	37	15/10/40
Davidson, L.A.C.	169, Ballards Road	45	15/10/40
Westlake, L.A.C.	169, Ballards Road	39	15/10/40
Doherty, Patrick	169, Ballards Road	28	15/10/40
Lodge, Mrs.	12, Vicarage Road	56	15/10/40
Bates, Mr.	169, Ballards Road	50	15/10/40
Bell, George	169, High Road	45	16/10/40
Johnson, Mr.	17, Digby Road	44	16/10/40
Tinton, Mr.	19, Rosslyn Avenue	33	16/10/40
Wallis, Alfred	30, Bedford Gdns., Hornchurch	30	17/10/40
Hogg, Mrs. Florence	515, Becontree Avenue	24	19/10/40
Clarke, Ellen	6, Broad Street	16	29/10/40
Clarke, Mrs. Agnes	6, Broad Street	50	29/10/40
Clarke, Dorothy	6, Broad Street	15	29/10/40
Castle, Albert	8, Broad Street	15	29/10/40
Castle, Victor	8, Broad Street	18	29/10/40
Castle, Frederick	8, Broad Street	20	29/10/40
Castle, Grace	8, Broad Street	11	29/10/40
Hall, Archie D.	19, Whalebone Avenue	12	30/10/40
Clifford, Herbert	60, Tantallon Road, Balham	35	2/11/40
Clifford, Mrs.	60, Tantallon Road, Balham	35	2/11/40
Holdbrook, Mrs. Lilian	11, Stanhope Gardens	23	3/11/40
Holdbrook, Frederick	11, Stanhope Gardens	31	3/11/40
Robinson, Edward	96, Auriel Avenue	1½	12/11/40
Jacks, John	96, Auriel Avenue	50	12/11/40
Robinson, Mrs. Elizabeth	96, Auriel Avenue	46	13/11/40
Jacks, Mrs. Elizabeth	96, Auriel Avenue	46	13/11/40
Annis, Philip	22, Boulton Road	18	16/11/40
Annis, Mrs. Rose	22, Boulton Road	45	16/11/40
Annis, Mrs. Esther	22, Boulton Road	56	16/11/40
Brooke, Mr.	24, Boulton Road	—	16/11/40
Brooks, Mrs.	24, Boulton Road	—	16/11/40
Anslow, George	17, Aldborough Road	65	9/12/40
Murphy, Walter	13, Aldborough Road	42	9/12/40
Sharpe, William	13, Aldborough Road	60	9/12/40
Bedford, Charles	100, Temple Avenue	43	22/12/40
Mitchell, Mrs.	111, Crescent Road	25	27/12/40
Morgan, Mrs.	45, Adelaide Gardens	35	27/12/40
Coppin, Jean	92, Maxey Road	10	19/ 1/41
Hennessey, Catherine	35, Cornshaw Road	52	16/ 3/41
Storey, Charles	37, Cornshaw Road	52	16/ 3/41
Church, Harold	33, Cornshaw Road	40	16/ 3/41
Burr, Ellen	1, Vine Cottages, Station Road	59	20/ 3/41
Barratt, Mrs. Elsie	110, Auriel Avenue	20	20/ 3/41
Rumsey, Mrs. Ethel	110, Auriel Avenue	49	20/ 3/41
Rumsey, Florence	110, Auriel Avenue	18	20/ 3/41
Purkiss, Eliza	112, Auriel Avenue	77	20/ 3/41
Purkiss, Ellen	112, Auriel Avenue	42	20/ 3/41
Purkiss, William	112, Auriel Avenue	78	20/ 3/41
Thompson, Frederick	112, Auriel Avenue	18	20/ 3/41
Thompson, Frederick	112, Auriel Avenue	42	20 /3/41
Thompson, Mary Ann	112, Auriel Avenue	44	20/ 3/41
Shepherd, Mr. J.	43, Norfolk Road, Upminster	38	20/ 3/41
Courtney, Mary	42, Wren Road	10	20/ 4/41
Courtney, Jean	42, Wren Road	7	20/ 4/41
Courtney, Donald	42, Wren Road	5	20/ 4/41

Name	Address	Age	Date of Death
Courtney, Mrs. Mary	42, Wren Road	41	20/ 4/41
Courtney, Robert	42, Wren Road	45	20/ 4/41
Nicholson, Nellie	531, Becontree Avenue	4	20/ 4/41
Nicholson, Edwin	531, Becontree Avenue	6	20/ 4/41
Nicholson, Mr. Edwin	531, Becontree Avenue	43	20/ 4/41
Buck, George	71, Baron Road	25	19/ 4/41
Smith, Mary Ann	40, Wren Road	39	20/ 4/41
Woodard, Alice	36, Alibon Road	25	19/ 4/41
Woodard, Thomas	36, Alibon Road	27	19/ 4/41
Smith, Helen	40, Wren Road	11	20/ 4/41
Smith, Irene May	40, Wren Road	9	20/ 4/41
*Kingdon, Edith May	16, Bonham Road	13	11/ 6/41
Chantley, William	90, Oval Road North	49	17/ 1/43
Curtis, George	153, Barking Road, East Ham	27	17/ 1/43
Coyle, Edward	165, Heathway	43	18/ 1/43
Hudson, Thomas	High Street, Doddington, March, Cambs.	33	3/ 3/43
Sammons, Mrs. Susan	42, Burlington Road	39	15/ 9/43
Newton, Peter	133, Valence Wood Road	3½	30/ 1/44
Newton, Mrs. Lilian	133, Valence Wood Road	32	2/ 2/44
Hodson, Florence	135, Valence Wood Road	38	30/ 1/44
Evans, Robert	160, Parsloes Avenue	65	21/ 2/44
Evans, Frances	160, Parsloes Avenue	72	21/ 2/44
Legon, Ald. William F.	58, Halbutt Street	48	18/ 3/44
Banks, Mrs. Nina	52, Cornwallis Road	20	21/ 4/44
Austin, Mrs. Elsie	17, Berther Road, Emerson Park, Hornchurch	42	16/ 6/44
Fry, Miss Lilian	16, Eustace Road, Chadwell Hth.	35	16/ 6/44
Woolmore, Margaret	10, Central Park Avenue	2	16/ 6/44
Herring, Miss Vera	4, Brendon Road	18	16/ 6/44
Duff, Gunner Michael	115, Arden Crescent, Gale Street	29	16/ 6/44
Beard, Jasmine	106, Temple Avenue	7	16/ 6/44
Waugh, Nurse Joyce	147, Hampton Road, Ilford	17	16/ 6/44
Barrett, Elizabeth	"North View," Cambridge Rd., Formby, Lancs.	28	16/ 6/44
Taylor, James	58, Comyns Road	51	3/ 7/44
Taylor, Alice	58, Comyns Road	49	3/ 7/44
Burkett, Mr. Henry	33, Rose Glen, Rush Green	43	9/ 7/44
Elliott, Mrs. Annie	33, Rose Glen, Rush Green	71	9/ 7/44
Gregson, Kenneth	48, Fanshawe Crescent	2½	13/ 7/44
Cosgrove, Walter	42, Fanshawe Crescent	52	13/ 7/44
Cosgrove, Mrs. Nellie	42, Fanshawe Crescent	46	13/ 7/44
Gradley, Mrs. Elsie	38, Fanshawe Crescent	42	13/ 7/44
Gradley, Lilian	38, Fanshawe Crescent	13	14/ 7/44
Garner, Robert	Soldier—Canadian Army	21	29/ 7/44
Wisher, Mrs. Maria	36, Tallis Grove, Charlton, S.E.	50	29/ 7/44
Gearing, Alice Louisa	37, Eliot Road	52	30/ 7/44
Horwill, Allen Keith	30, Stockdale Gardens	2½ mths.	1/ 8/44
Martin, Mr.	402, Whalebone Lane North	42	3/ 8/44
Davis, George Raymond	228, Oval Road North	7	3/ 8/44
Elliott, Anthony James	29, Gorseway, Rush Green	12	5/ 8/44
Walklin, Arthur	7, Ashton Gardens	53	31/ 8/44
Bennett, Mrs. Catherine	85, East Road	60	31/ 8/44
Moy, Alfred	83, East Road	40	31/ 8/44
Harding, Mrs. Janet (Sgt. (W.A.A.F.)	122, Lymington Road	24	5/11/44

*This child was killed whilst evacuated and was brought back to Dagenham for burial. She was living in a remote hamlet near Baddesley Ensor (Shrewley Common) and a bomber, possibly in trouble, dropped a stray bomb on farm cottages far from any other habitation.

Name	Address	Age	Date of Death
Hall, Benjamin	183, Osborne Square	52	11/11/44
Hall, Mrs. Ada	183, Osborne Square	55	11/11/44
Hudson-Parker, George	183, Osborne Square	23	11/11/44
Hudson-Parker, Kathleen	183, Osborne Square	23	11/11/44
Hudson-Parker, Patricia	183, Osborne Square	1½	11/11/44
Cooper, Mr. Arthur	70, Halbutt Street	61	11/11/44
Looker, Robert	76, Halbutt Street	16	11/11/44
Fewell, John	Wheel Farm Cottage, Dagenham Road	77	18/11/44
Fewell, Jane	Wheel Farm Cottage, Dagenham Road	61	18/11/44
George, John Owen	5, Woodlands Ave., Chad. Hth.	60	7/ 1/45
Jones, Patience May	5, Woodlands Ave., Chad. Hth.	31	7/ 1/45
Jones, Elizabeth Ann	5, Woodlands Ave., Chad. Hth.	3½	7/ 1/45
Scales, Charles Henry	1, Woodlands Ave., Chad. Hth.	30	7/ 1/45
Gardner, Ethel May	7, Woodlands Ave., Chad. Hth.	58	7/ 1/45
Leader, Beatrice May	3, Woodlands Ave., Chad. Hth.	51	7/ 1/45
Leader, George Alfred	3, Woodlands Ave., Chad. Hth.	50	7/ 1/45
Woods, William George	153, Rosebank Avenue, Elm Park	36	23/ 1/45
Hackett, Philip	19, Glenwood Avenue, Rainham	31	23/ 1/45
Mather, Jeanette	7, Victoria Cottages	7	23/ 1/45
Martin, Alfred George	2, Victoria Cottages	53	23/ 1/45
Stevens, Mary Ormond	147, Groveway	48	8/ 2/45
Truscott, William	125, Eyhurst Avenue, Elm Park	35	24/ 2/45
West, Ada Lena	126, Sterry Road	32	24/ 2/45

THE BOROUGH COUNCIL, 1939 — 1945

MAYORS

A. F. J. Chorley, J.P., E.C.C.	Elected in	1938 and	1939
R. J. D. Clack, J.P.	,,	1940 ,,	1941
L. F. Evans, (Mrs.), M.B.E., J.P., E.C.C.	,,	1942 ,,	1943
Fred Brown, J.P.	,,	1944	
F. G. Thomas, J.P.	,,	1945	

DEPUTY MAYORS

B. H. Saunders	Elected in	1938	
R. J. D. Clack, J.P.	,,	1939	
L. F. Evans (Mrs.), M.B.E., J.P., E.C.C.	,,	1940 and	1941
Fred Brown, J.P.	,,	1942 ,,	1943
F. G. Thomas, J.P.	,,	1944	
A. F. J. Chorley, J.P., E.C.C.	,,	1945	

MEMBERS OF THE COUNCIL WHO SERVED (WITH THE MAYORS AND DEPUTY MAYORS) EITHER FOR THE WHOLE OR THE GREATER PART OF THE YEARS 1939–45

Andrews, Coun. J. R.
Banks, Ald. (Mrs.) A. L.
*Bellamy, Ald. W. E., J.P.
*Brown, Coun. D. E.
*Burridge, Coun. J. W.
*Butters, Coun. A. A.
Cain, Coun. W. T.
Deeks, Coun. S. W.
Edwards, Coun. E.
Gibbs, Coun. Dr. A. G.
Grindrod, Coun. F. T.
Hennem, Ald. E. E.
Hollidge, Coun. J. P. P.
Legon, Ald. W. F. (*killed by enemy action*)
Lyons, Coun. H. L.
Markham, Ald. W. C.

Marley, Ald. (Mrs.) M. E., J.P.
*Minchin, Ald. P. J.
*Munn, Coun. J. E.
Neish, Coun. (Mrs.) J.
Murell, Coun. R. G.
Osborne, Coun. E.
Perfect, Coun. F. S.
Prendergast, Coun. (Mrs.) A. E.
Reddy, Coun. (Mrs.) E. S.
Reddy, Coun. M.
Rogers, Coun. A.
Rogers, Coun. (Mrs.) F. L. M.
Saywood, Coun. E. R.
Thomas, Coun. (Mrs.) A. R.
Thorneycroft, Ald. C. A.
Warren, Coun. (Mrs.) M.

* Served in the Forces.

DANGER OVER DAGENHAM

CHAPTER ONE

DAGENHAM AT WAR—
A RECAPITULATION

THE preamble to this account of Dagenham at War—a recapitulation of war work within the Borough—commences with the passing of the Air Raid Precautions Act which became law in December, 1937. This does not mean that Civil Defence alone is the theme of this account, but this Act was the first sign in local affairs of the war that was to follow.

Under the 1937 Act the Essex County Council (not the Borough) was instructed to prepare general Air Raid Precautions Schemes in collaboration with the Borough. This was the start of it all. The Fire Brigade Act of 1938 placed upon the Borough Council the duty of preparing Air Raid Fire Precautions schemes for the Secretary of State and to complete the Statutory side of these matters the Civil Defence Act of 1939 considerably widened the air raid precautions generally, including the provision for the evacuation of dangerous areas.

That is the general statutory background of Civil Defence. Little more need be said of it as we are mainly concerned with the war from the citizen's point of view.

In March, 1938, following the Act of the previous December, the Council interviewed Essex County Council officials on an A.R.P. Scheme for Dagenham and, in the same month, submitted their Fire Precautions Scheme direct to the Home Office. The reader will gather that no time was being lost in organising local Civil Defence. (In the midst of all this, the Urban District became a Borough—an event much hoped for and great plans were in view for celebrating it.) After the County conference in March, 1938, the first A.R.P. officer was appointed and a general Civil Defence Scheme was placed on paper.

The main outline of the scheme was briefly as follows. Civil Defence was divided into three principal sections. These were the Medical services, the Rescue services and the Wardens service. The Medical service covered first aid, ambulances and the mortuary. Hospitals were under the direct control of the Ministry of Health. Rescue service embraced three depots staffed with light and heavy rescue gangs working under instructions from the central control room. Each depot was provided with decontamination buildings for gas attacks. The Wardens service covered wardens posts, shelter accommodation and the original fire guard service. The fourth arm, the Fire Service, worked under its own control although under central control and trained its own A.F.S. recruits and staff. This organisation was later taken over entirely by the Home Office. The broad picture in 1938 was these four main services of Civil Defence— Medical, Rescue, Wardens and Fire Services all unified by Central Control.

I will not weary the reader with the larger organisation of group control. Briefly, Dagenham belonged to Group 7, whose headquarters were in the New Town Hall at Walthamstow. All air raid incidents were reported to Group who were responsible for the co-ordination of all services and for obtaining aid from neighbouring authorities when one authority was hard pressed. The summit of the organisation was the Essex County Council and the Regional Commissioner who decided major questions of policy.

Between March, 1938 and Munich, in September of that year, the first volunteer recruits for A.R.P. services were enlisted and got into training. A recruiting campaign was conducted—numerous appeals were made from cinema stages but there was no great rush to serve until Munich. That woke everybody up. Over 100,000 gas masks were distributed within a few days—the sandbagging—the feverish tearing work of getting up protection—the question of shelter accommodation—it was a week of all work and not very much talk.

Our poor Borough Charter celebrations were abandoned, except for a Charter Ball held after the Munich Agreement. It seemed a celebration at the time.

After Munich week our Civil Defence work assumed a more serious aspect. Training and recruiting of volunteers went ahead. There was mainly training of wardens, anti-gas gangs and A.F.S. auxiliaries. By August, 1939, Air Raid Precautions looked like ceasing to be a precautionary measure and Government instructions were received to get on with building decontamination premises, shelters, control centres and other building requirements. In the meantime, the question of evacuation had been dealt with—Dagenham made a vigorous protest at being excluded from the evacuation scheme and in the June before the outbreak of war was included among the areas to be evacuated. This added another piece to the pattern of A.R.P. When war broke out we were not entirely prepared—nobody was, but we were well on the way. The Central Control room was ready, so were the three dispersed depots. First aid posts were manned, the fire service called-up its auxiliaries, and the main scheme was in being. The framework required clothing but it was there and capable of carrying out its function.

That was the situation at the declaration of war on Sunday, 3rd September, 1939. One part of Civil Defence had already been put into operation. Roughly 17,000 mothers and children with teachers and escorts had been evacuated to Norfolk and Suffolk.

September and October of 1939 were weeks of unceasing activity day and night. Buildings, shelters, staffing (paid staff now, not volunteers, although many volunteers, particularly among wardens, served throughout or for part of the war). Control centre, shadow control centre, depots, first aid posts, decontamination, anti-gas, fire services, and the pattern of the Civil Defence services formed itself into a recognisable scheme.

The Emergency Committee of the Borough Council met daily. The ordinary reader—the citizen—may hardly believe this. But it was so, it met daily and remained in session all day—even on Sundays although this was avoided if possible. This went on for some long time and the Committee only ceased to meet daily when every detail of Civil Defence was organised and in good working order.

The year of "phoney" war was useful that in that degree it gave us time to prepare. The story of each individual service will appear later. The actual incidents of the war, in part taken from the Controller's day-to-day record, will give a brief résumé of air warfare over Dagenham.

Essex had two early reminders of air warfare. A Heinkel with two mines on board came down in Clacton on 30th April, 1940. One mine exploded and did a lot of damage. On the 24th May following, a high explosive bomb dropped at Wickford, not many miles away. By the time the attack on London started we had a fair notion of what to expect.

The first high explosive bomb fell in Dagenham on 26th July, 1940, in Raydons Road opposite the wardens' post. There were only three slight casualties, although fifty-four houses were damaged, six seriously. "Casualties were slight" —that is going to be the theme of this part of the report. Study the bomb map and see where bombs and other things fell. Dagenham, so uncrowded in its layout and surrounded by open ground, was saved from a heavy casualty list by this fact.

The first bomb on the 26th July, 1940, a month without an incident and the next on 24th August with two bombs in Chadwell Heath and the first incendiaries, no casualties. The following day ten bombs dropped mainly in Rush Green —three slight casualties. It is impossible to go on with this day-to-day record—scarcely a night passed without an incident or more.

Dagenham being on the outer perimeter of London, noise was terrific. Gunfire commenced at dusk and ended at dawn. Each one of us met this nightly tornado of noise in his own way. I remember Nat Gubbins' immortal remark, "Ear plugs for the poor, plenty of wallop for the rich." The reader may not realise that on the outer fringes of London there was no escaping the noise. No deep tubes, no shelter nor rest from it. Yet we slept, or most of us did.

Examples of good and bad nights are shown in the Controller's reports. On the 4th September, sixteen bombs fell on open ground near the river, two failed to explode— five slight casualties. Four days later twenty-three bombs (six unexploded) and eight ack-ack shells landed round the Chadwell Heath gunsite—casualties slight. The first fatal casualty occurred on 15th September at Baron Road—the first serious incident from a casualty point of view. Two days later the parachute mines arrived. One came to rest in the centre of New Road outside the Princess Cinema. This did not explode and was successfully dismantled by an Army officer clad only in underwear. The second came to rest in an upstairs room of a house after penetrating the roof, leaving the parachute draping the roof and walls. This eventually exploded when a naval squad were attempting to render it harmless. For them there was no grave—not even that of the sea. Four days later two bombs (Cartwright and Surrey Roads) killed seven people—damage very considerable. The following night (20th September) we captured thirty-nine incendiaries with their containers. All unexploded. Three days later two hundred more landed round the " Merry Fiddlers "—they did explode. On September 22nd and 23rd there were more deaths. Two whole families were killed on the 23rd and the same night a parachute mine landed in Western Avenue. By the end of September, twenty-four people had been killed, one hundred and eight injured and one thousand nine hundred and ninety-three houses had been damaged—over four hundred badly. October opened badly —on the 2nd seven deaths, five in Connor Road (that was, I think, the bomb disposal squad—all were lost getting out an unexploded bomb). On the 5th of the same month, eighteen were killed in Thompson Road, eight of these belonging to one family. One bomb landed in the midst of a cluster of Anderson shelters grouped at the bottom of converging gardens. It was the worst incident we had. The sole survivor of one of the families was a very young boy evacuated to Cornwall. An aged relative from another part of London claimed him, and refusing all offers of help, cheerfully added her little kinsman to her own burdens. Six people in Windsor Road were killed the same night. On the 13th, ten bombs in a string fell—across Hainault Forest— excellent spot. Two nights later five deaths occurred in Vicarage Road and seven in Ballards Road. On the 21st, Hainault Forest again, but eighteen bombs this time—nothing to report. October 28th, seven dead in Broad Street and by the end of the month casualties amounted to seventy-nine killed, two hundred and sixty-eight injured and nearly four thousand houses damaged. November was a better month —thirteen killed. Incidents were fewer in number, although the noise never diminished for one night.

Christmas of 1940 and two nights of complete quiet—not a siren, not a gun. It was the " gentle sleep from heaven that slid into my soul." The Rest Centre at Halbutt Street was full of homeless people but they celebrated Christmas in good style.

That break did us all a power of good. But it did not last—on the night of 27th December, four parachute mines were dropped, two by Central Park and two in Chadwell Heath. Damage was terrible and, of course, there were casualties. To add to the night's troubles, we had some incendiaries as well. We had a spell without a single incident until 5th January, 1941, and then we had two nights of incidents (but again six bombs in Hainault Forest—a lot of trouble for such a result). Six more nights without an incident, and then three more H.E. bombs all over the place. The blitz was quietening off a lot by this time—bombs and incendiaries arrived but not every night, although there was still a lot of noise throughout the nights. We escaped further fatal casualties until 14th March when three persons were killed by a bomb in Cornshaw Road. Six days later a parachute mine landed in Auriel Avenue—ten were killed, forty-two injured, and although the mine landed almost in the fields, the immediate damage was bad.

On the 17th April an incident at the Ford Motor factory occurred which I relate by quotation :—

" Every man employed in the Power House knew that a 250 lb. bomb properly placed would probably be enough to destroy them all, for they were working among boilers each with a pressure of 1,200 lbs. to the square inch, and 40,000 horse-power turbines turning at 3,000 revolutions a minute, housed in buildings whose walls and ceilings contained cables carrying 11,000 volts, near which ran water and gas mains. To these potential sources of danger had to be added many thousands of gallons of highly inflammable oil.

" At 1.43 a.m. on the 17th April, 1941, it happened. That night the factory was under particularly heavy air attack, and was constantly hit by incendiaries and presently by three high explosive bombs. It became necessary for the Controller to issue an order plunging the works into total darkness for some hours, and this made the task of those working in the Power House even more difficult. They carried on, however, until a shower of incendiaries pierced the roof and fell among the machinery, one dropping between the high and low pressure cylinders of No. 1 turbine. Norman Halliburton pulled it away with his bare hands, and with his mate, Henry Craig Mack, began to extinguish it, when it exploded, wounding Halliburton in the stomach and removing two of Mack's toes. James Gordon and Alexander Hector McAllister, who ran to their assistance, were also wounded, but the bombs were put out and the turbine remained unscathed. It is such men as these who, all over the country, remaining at their posts at the height of danger night after night, saved England." (From " Ford at War " by Hilary St. George Saunders.)

That is another view point of this nightly warfare, the men and women who worked because their work was vital— their cover often a blackened glass roof. There were many such men and women in Dagenham, their records unwritten. How or when they rested I don't know because the days were not free from enemy action. I quote again from the same source :—

" An instance of the determination of all to make certain that never for a moment would the machinery in the Power House, on the proper working of which the whole factory depended, be allowed to get out of hand, is afforded by the conduct of Cornelius Sheehan and John Maurice Finch on that night in April when No. 1 turbine was so nearly destroyed. The two men were furnace workers, and with other members of their department they remained at their posts and maintained the heat treatment furnace in full production, and this, though they were well aware of what had happened in the turbine room close by. Such devotion to duty would be worthy of remark in the conduct of a soldier on the battlefield, subject though he is to military discipline and fortified by military tradition; but in these two workers, ordinary citizens of a free country with shelter available and at hand, it deserves the highest praise."

To return to the daily record, an unlucky hit in Alibon Road on 19th April caused two fatal casualties. A bomb fell in Baron Road and a mine landed in Chadwell Heath. The following night three mines landed and a number of bombs. There were deaths in Valence Avenue (damage also to Valence House and Library) and in Wren Road—eleven in all with other casualties. A mine that landed in Gordon Road, Chadwell Heath that night damaged six hundred and twenty houses, but casualties were slight. On the 23rd April another mine in the Forest—damage nil, casualties nil. That was almost the last thing to fall in the Borough in that year. The first blitz was over and done with. We had been pretty lucky compared with other parts of London, or even our immediate neighbours. Casualties were as follows :—

Dead	127
Seriously injured	243
Slightly injured	471
Damage to property :—	
Demolished houses	132
Incapable of repair	357
Very badly damaged, but repairable . .	2,147
Damaged badly, but habitable . . .	1,142
Slightly damaged	8,883
No. of bombs (H.E.)	429
„ bombs (unexploded)	117
„ shells	13
„ shells (unexploded)	28
„ parachute mines	24
„ parachute mines (unexploded) . .	1
„ oil bombs	31

That was round number one.

Despite this story of damage and casualties, life went on as usual. War work was in full swing. Damage to local factories (including Ford's and the riverside works) had not been severe except for a big hit at Briggs Motor Bodies and a bomb on the main gate of Sterling Engineering. All the services had worked smoothly—Medical—Rescue—Rest

Centres—Evacuation—Rehousing. Their full story is told separately in this account. One bomb had hit the Civic Centre, but only just, and another fell outside. The bomb that hit the Civic Centre caused one casualty. It hit the extreme south end of the building, carrying away an overhanging canopy, and finished up somewhere in the basement. The senior staff in the Control Room always consisted of permanent Council staff who took their turn night by night on Control Room duties. On this occasion the Building Inspector was on duty. After the dust settled and everyone had sorted themselves out, he departed outside the building to inspect the damage. It was extremely dark and in the darkness he fell flat on his face into the ice-cold water of an ornamental pond. Otherwise there were no casualties.

Central Control had never ceased to function for one hour in the twenty-four or one day in the week. After the mine that fell in the Forest on 23rd June, 1941, there is no entry in the Controller's daily report until July, 1942, when some minor enemy activity commenced. There are entries in the report for September, October and December. Not very serious. A bad incident with an A.A. shell outside the " Admiral Vernon " on 17th January, 1943—three killed, fourteen injured. There are quite a number of shell incidents after this, but on the 3rd March the new incendiaries appeared —the phosphorus bombs. Halbutt Street was unlucky this time. After that month of March was another quiet period. Apart from ack-ack shells, nothing landed until January, 1944, when we had more phosphorus bombs with casualties and damage. Numerous incendiaries the same night, also. 31st January, again in the Forest—phosphorous this time. No incident worth comment occurred until 20th February, 1944, when three bombs came down by Fanshawe Crescent. Two deaths and casualties. Three large bombs by Whalebone Lane and Eastern Avenue accomplished nothing, but ruined a rhubarb patch and made a hole in the road. In incidents after this there is a recurring note of fire raising—incendiaries and phosphorus bombs. That didn't do much harm. Some missed May & Baker's chemical works although their canteen caught it. They still went on making M and B and thousands of other things as well, including the substitute for quinine (Malaya was in Jap hands).

On the 16th June a novel missile landed behind May &
Baker's and within their grounds. Fly bomb number one—
the first entry for this missile in the Controller's log. The
same night one hit the Rush Green Hospital—eight patients
and nurses killed—injuries and damage. This hospital—
a peace-time Isolation Hospital—is built in single storey
pavilions. No protection for doctors, nurses or patients, but
it never ceased to function in its war-time capacity as an
emergency hospital. The last fly bomb fell on 26th March,
1945, in some gravel pits at Marks Gate. Thirty-two fly
bombs landed in Dagenham. They caused twenty-four
deaths—not one for each fly bomb—but damage was terrific.
One of the worst incidents, on 11th November, was between
Halbutt Street and Osborne Square. Seven died, fifty-eight
were injured, seventeen houses wrecked beyond repair, three
hundred and ninety very badly damaged and six hundred and
forty-eight damaged one way or another. Fanshawe Crescent
on the 13th July previously was a bad incident, almost equal
to that just named.

But we had a lot of luck as the total casualties to fly bombs
show. " The battle of the fly bomb is won " sounded like a
benediction in a broadcast not yet forgotten. I still remember
the first rocket that fell in England. That was on September
8th, 1944 at 6.35 p.m. and it landed in a wood at Epping
Upland not far from Epping and not many miles from
Dagenham as sound travels. Four days later on Tuesday,
12th September the first rocket dropped in Dagenham. It
fell at breakfast time outside the Special School, Heathway,
where a number of very small children were at breakfast.
The building was a single storey built of wood and glass.
Not one child was hurt.

In all we had twenty rockets—fourth on the list for number
seven London civil defence area. Ilford, our neighbour,
was number one. Again our luck held. Damage was very
large but number of deaths was eighteen. One fell on 7th
March behind the " Eastbrook " where there was a crowded
dance hall. No deaths. The same morning one fell opposite
Briggs Motor Bodies killing three pedestrians. Twenty yards
shorter in its flight and the factory with thousands of workers
would have received a direct hit. The worst incident was at

Woodlands Avenue, Chadwell Heath on January 7th. Seven were killed, seventy-five injured and tremendous damage done to houses. The rocket had one consolation—there were no sirens and no gunfire. It was a terrible weapon. I saw one explode under a lowering grey sky heavy with rain. The burst of flame against the grey clouds, scarlet and orange and lasting an appreciable time, was an unforgettable sight. One further reflection, listening to the beginning of midnight mass broadcast from the solemn quiet of Buckfast Abbey. A rocket exploded in the Forest (without casualties or damage) but the noise reverberated, roared and remained almost suspended in the midnight air. The all unknowing choir continued their ageless chant " Et in terra pax hominibus "—" peace on earth to men of good will."

The last rocket was an air burst over the Chadwell Heath gunsite—the last missile of all was a fly bomb that landed in some gravel pits at Marks Gate on 26th March, 1945.

The last entry in the Controller's log records the finding of an unexploded bomb on 21st April, 1945—believed to have fallen during the blitz of 1941. It was found (oh happy place) in Hainault Forest.

The Controller's log sums up air warfare in Dagenham with a final casting of figures. Here they are :—

CASUALTIES (no separate figures for bombs, fly bombs and rockets are allowed).

Dead	190
Seriously injured	567
Injured	1,060
Total	1,817

DAMAGE

Houses totally demolished	188
„ beyond repair and taken down	419
„ badly damaged. Not inhabitable but repairable	1,952
„ badly damaged but inhabitable and repairable	5,267
„ lightly damaged	17,426
Total	25,252

NUMBER OF INCIDENTS	.	.	.	913

FALLING BODIES

Bombs (H.E. which exploded)	.	.	.	467
Bombs (unexploded) .	.	.	.	146
Parachute mines (exploded)	.	.	.	24
Parachute mines (unexploded)	.	.	.	6
Fly bombs .	.	.	.	.	.	33
Rockets .	.	.	.	.	.	20

Fire raisers—

Incendiaries (too many to count)				
Phosphorus bombs	.	.	.	.	18
Oil bombs (exploded)	.	.	.	.	32
Oil bombs (unexploded) .	.	.	.	1
Parachute flares (intact) .	.	.	.	3

To which must be added non-German missiles :—

A.A. shells (exploded)	.	.	.	.	76
A.A. shells (unexploded)	.	.	.	.	74
Cannon shells .	.	.	.	.	.	7

That's the end of that side of the story. Each service will now tell its own story—industry and agriculture will display their part in the war and, finally, that valuable footnote to war work the Women's Voluntary Services, Forces House and the work of National Savings.

Destruction around May and Baker after it was bombed 16th October 1940

LBBD Archives at Valence House (BD4/889)

Ford's Motor Company works exterior following a bombing raid. 1939 - 1945

LBBD Archives at Valence House (DS913)

CHAPTER TWO

CIVIL DEFENCE
CONTROL SERVICES

DURING the whole period of the war, the Control Room and Report Centre has been in the basement of the Civic Centre. The Control Room was the nerve centre of the whole complicated system of Civil Defence, and was in direct communication with Group Seven Headquarters, Police and Fire Service. Here, in addition to the staff to deal with reports coming in and instructions going out, were the Officers controlling all the Services, and on their decisions (which had to be made rapidly), depended the success of " operations " and the welfare of all persons affected by incidents.

In the early days of the war, before the lessons which came with bombing were learned, the method of "one person— one job " was the rule ; but it was very soon found that duties, so far as telephonists and records clerks were concerned, had to be interchangeable. The Controller had always to be on duty, or to have an efficient deputy to deal with all the wide range of subjects on which decisions had to be made. He had at any time to deal with up to thirty different services, all wishing to get to work as quickly as possible, and each in his own view holding priority. Firstly it was obvious that the Rescue and Casualty Services must be sent out—if they were not already on their way. This would be the procedure if the local Depot knew that an incident had occurred and also knew its location. In such a case (a development of the fly bomb period), Control would be notified later, and by this means valuable minutes were saved in getting to incidents. The day and night staff at Control Centre were the Controller on duty, Borough Engineer's representative, Medical Officer's representative, Officer-in-charge of Control Room, Operations Clerks, Records Clerk, Message Clerk, and six Telephonists augmented after 1942 with part-time Telephonists. Control had telephone communication with Wardens Posts, First Aid Posts, Depots, Mortuary, Police, N.F.S., Electricity, Gas and Water Companies, etc., and the number of telephones to be

manned in the Control Room was 23.   It seemed on occasions
that they were all ringing at once.

When several incidents occurred in one raid, work was
heavy as every message had to be taken down, every instruction
sent out, utility services had to be contacted and advised,
Group H.Q. and sometimes London Region had to be notified
of progress or requests for reinforcements from other Boroughs.
Further, in the middle of the raid, a request was often received
to send reinforcements which were badly needed to other
Boroughs.   The Controller had always to keep in mind the
possibility of further trouble developing, of potential calls for
assistance from other authorities, and a clear picture of the
situation so far as his own incidents were concerned.

Control Room staff had to work at high pressure both
during and after the raid had ceased, in order to collate the
information they received and pass it on to higher authority.
This had to be done during the course of the raid, and the
final work cleared up and returns made as soon after as possible.

A word picture of Control Room in action might read—
an incident with phone bells ringing, all hustle and bustle but
quiet voices giving orders ;   everyone realising that much
depended on him or her.   The care of the homeless, casualties
and injured, the recovery of what was left, roads to be cleared
in order that workers could get to work and not hold up
production and transport.   A further incident ;   a request to
Group Headquarters for assistance and then the transfer of
ambulances to other sites.   A report comes in that more Rescue
Parties are wanted and Rest Centres must be opened.   Gas
and water mains have burst and fires have been started.   The
Controller asks, " How many parties have we at a particular
incident ? "   The system of working shows at once what we
had there.   A telephonist taking a message hears that her own
home has gone but she still carries on.   A request is made
for canteens to go out and the mortuary van is required.   A
new type of bomb is reported by the Wardens Service and
immediate reports are made to Headquarters.   The Bomb
Disposal section of the Royal Engineers must be told of the
locality of unexploded H.E.'s.   Suspicious holes in back
gardens are noted for investigation.   The Rescue Officer
comes in from the incident—dirty and muddy—to say that

his parties have drawn off till dawn, but we must go on and get it cleared up, Jerry may be back. So we start all over again.

When the possibility of invasion appeared, an Invasion Defence Scheme was prepared and a Military Liaison Officer was appointed to Control to deal with military matters. Invasion did not come, but that made no difference to the Invasion Defence Scheme—to be dealt with in another section.

Then came the preparations for D Day that coincided with our fly bomb period. We were assigned our part in the great invasion. We knew that our duty was to keep communications open. The convoys had to get through even if we had to work with short staff on bombing incidents. Fly bombs arrived during this time day and night and later rockets.

Control working at all times was never seen at work. There were times when there was no enemy action but Control was fully manned day and night. It worked through various phases—bombs, incendiary bombs, explosive incendiaries, incendiaries in containers, heavier bombs, parachute mines, flares, oil bombs, phosphorus bombs, rocket shells, A.A. shells, fly bombs and rockets and unexploded bombs.

In an earlier chapter details of bombs, damage and casualties have been given. These comprised nine hundred and thirteen incidents. Each and every one of these was dealt with in the Control Room and the information sifted and collated, the services put into motion and the hundred and one details of an " incident." This was the hidden part of Civil Defence and in reality its nerve centre.

Wardens Service

The Wardens Service was first recruited and trained in the early part of 1938 and in common with the whole Civil Defence Service this was considerably accelerated after Munich. They were then entirely unpaid volunteers and many part-time wardens maintained their voluntary duties throughout the war. The outbreak of war necessitated the appointment of full-time wardens.

A long period of inactivity followed the outbreak of war enlivened only by the periods of training, the issue of uniform overalls and the building of wardens posts. A period followed of yellow warnings very often several times a night, which brought both whole and part-time men alike along to posts for the " standby." Almost inevitably on arrival at the Posts they would learn that the " white " had been received but they insisted on being called out

Warnings were yellow (raiders on the way), purple (raiders returning air raid near at hand), red (raiders overhead) and white (" all clear ").

The Battle of Britain (Summer 1940) did not affect the Borough at all but the Wardens got their first experience of persuading the public to get into shelters.

By this time the permanent posts had been erected each with a Post Warden, generally in a whole-time capacity, responsible for a surrounding area of approximately half-a-mile radius. He had a complete record of the inhabitants of each area which was retained in each post so that when the first bomb fell in the Borough the Service was able to go into action with the other C.D. Services, primed well with :—

(1) A complete knowledge of the area involved for reporting and operational purposes.

(2) A knowledge of the names and numbers of the unfortunate occupants of the houses affected by the bombing. This knowledge was necessary to the Rescue Service on their arrival.

Throughout the blitz many lessons were learnt and innovations were introduced, chief among them being the introduction of Incident Officers, senior officers of the Wardens Service who were Regionally trained to co-ordinate and supervise the different services present at incidents. This important feature of a Warden's duty was so enthusiastically taken up that by 1943 there were some 150 Wardens trained to act as Incident Officers, and this proved itself to be a valuable asset particularly when the V Bomb era arrived for then the trained officer was on the spot ready to take charge.

During the first blitz when the authorities realised that pavement and trench shelters were being used for all night sheltering, these were bunked and heated. The warden added shelter control to his duties. Another useful little job was blackout patrol—loitering round his section for unobscured lights before the police came on the scene. A kindness that was often mistaken by the householder.

Many unexploded bombs fell during these raiding periods and the Bomb Disposal Units were overwhelmed with reports of such, many of them of an exaggerated or spurious nature. It was decided to train a number of Wardens and Police in each Authority to undertake the duties of investigating, categorising, and taking the necessary precautions, prior to the B.D.S. being called in. Six officers were chosen and duly took their training at the Duke of York's Headquarters, Chelsea, under the supervision of R.E. Instructors. All passed their examinations and became Q.R.C.D. Officers (Qualified Bomb Reconnaissance Civil Defence) and put in a good job of work in the subsequent bombings which we endured in Dagenham.

A big drive was undertaken in 1942 to increase the Housewives' service membership of the W.V.S. This campaign made at the request of the Centre Organiser was so enthusiastically taken up, that by the end of 1942 the numbers jumped from 300 to nearly 2,000. The training of the ladies followed usually undertaken by the District and Post Wardens, but that this had its reward was evidenced especially in the V weapon attacks which came in the latter stages of the war, when many of these volunteers worked side by side with the Wardens manning the Enquiry Points, the mobile kitchens and the Rest Centres.

During all this time we were being subjected spasmodically to night attacks and many bombs fell in and around the Borough. In order to give the Part-timers as much rest as possible, annexes were built on the Wardens Posts, bunks and blankets installed therein, all posts being manned at night with a whole-timer, usually the Post or Deputy Post Warden and one or two part-time personnel.

About this time in the war instructions were issued to overhaul the anti-gas organisation. Our activities in enemy skies, it was thought, might bring some unpleasant reprisals. A number of Wardens were trained to augment the staffs of the Public Cleansing Posts. Anti-gas clothing was thoroughly inspected. All civilian respirators were inspected and put into repair. A special point was made at the schools where systematic examinations and repairing of gas masks was carried out. At this time the enemy increased their use of anti-personnel bombs. No more than a few pounds in weight these S.D.2's (as they were termed) were dropped in clusters and contained various types of time and anti-handling fuzes, having a killing range of many yards. They presented a very difficult proposition to deal with and so a technique of searching for these weapons was developed by the B.D.S. who passed it over to the Q.R.C.D.'s who trained the wardens service in methods of detection.

A fairly quiet period brought us to " D " Day and we had " Military Roads " running through the Borough which demanded a continuous surveillance. In consequence, we had to bring back some whole-time Wardens from industry whence they had been transferred during a quiet spell in 1942.

The rest of May and the early part of June passed off without any aerial activity over the country on the part of the Luftwaffe, and as by now our Army was firmly established on the Continent, it was too late for them to stem the Invasion by bombing the embarkation ports and the roads leading to them, the tension which had been endured by the Personnel was somewhat lifted.

New weapons meant, especially in this case, an overhaul and re-adjustment in the method of dealing with them. These bombs could be seen approaching and diving and so the C.D. Services were called in to take a hand in reporting the place of their fall. A watch was maintained from all Wardens Posts, Depots, N.F.S. Stations, and this continued during all Alert periods which followed monotonously night and day until the last week in August.

The advantage of the plan was the simultaneous arrival of all services within a few minutes of the explosion on the site of the incident. All the services now included the N.F.S. who turned out with soldiers also, when available, to lend a hand in the wide area of damage. It was a tough time for the services and relief and help was directed from more than one source. The Army came in to help with no uncertain will. In some areas they gave almost the whole of the C.D. services a break. Twenty-five Wardens came down from Scotland as volunteers to ease the situation. Apparently an enjoyable visit for guests and locals. They came in at the tail end and only one flying bomb fell during their stay. This fell at East Road, Chadwell Heath in the morning of the 31st August (one very pathetic casualty, a small child was blinded for life).

The Wardens' Service, at the apparent cessation of bombing, began to think about the future and those who were recalled, to contemplate a return to industry. However, on the 12th September a rocket (at that time not referred to as such or as anything) fell by the Heathway Special School.

The story of the Rocket episode has been told already elsewhere. We had got so used to damage with the flying bombs that the increased area of damage by rockets hardly caused any surprise. Casualties were light fortunately and no very sad incidents. Factories and congested places all escaped, although the great Ford Factory had two very narrow shaves and so had May & Baker.

One District Warden attended the Royal Parade in Hyde Park for the grand farewell to the Civil Defence services on June 10th, 1945. When due reflection is made on war services for Civilian Defence the Warden is seen in his true place as the backbone of the service.

Gas Identification

The primary duty of the Gas Identification Service was to provide skilled technical advice and assistance to other sections of Civil Defence on the identity and properties of any war gas used, its dangers and their extent, defence measures to be taken, its " decontamination," or any special problems arising and, of course, to maintain the utmost vigilance for any new types of chemical warfare agent and ensure that they were promptly investigated.

Recruitment of this service was on a very small scale at first, and never very great—one Gas Identification Officer per 30,000 population was the basis—Dagenham's allotment being three G.I.O.'s.

They were recruited mainly from the ranks of experienced works chemists, with degrees in chemistry. Service was voluntary throughout. They had the backing of the technical guidance of 12 Senior Gas Advisers operating at Regional level, drawn from university staffs at convenient centres.

These centres also provided special training courses in which war gases, their properties and characteristics, were studied in the fullest detail. Perhaps the feature of their training course that will live longest in the memory of G.I.O.'s is the many and various disagreeable symptoms inflicted on their person by the variety of war gases they were dosed with during its progress.

In Dagenham the three G.I.O.'s originally appointed were recruited in September, 1939, and all had received their special training and equipment by January, 1940. At a later date three Assistant G.I.O.'s were recruited. A trained assistant was to accompany each G.I.O. on " field work " and assist him in making the precise and careful investigations it was his duty to make under the difficult conditions that would always surround an actual incident.

Still later—as the university centres completed their task of training the main body of G.I.O.'s—large factories were allotted their own fully trained G.I.O., selected from their own staffs, who could better assess the special problems of a gas incident in their own industrial concerns, and relieve the Local Authorities' G.I.O.'s of this burden. Meetings, discussions, refresher courses and practices were frequently held, at district, group and regional levels. Constant improvement in the methods of investigation of incidents were made ; new types of war gas were introduced and duly studied.

Though no hostile use of war gases was ever made—and in Dagenham not one authentic call was made for a G.I.O. to examine a " suspected gas " incident—quite a substantial number of real calls on G.I.O.'s were made to examine suspected gas incidents in other parts of the country. Some were found to be of industrial origin. Two were found to be due to fermenting crops in stack. One proved to be carbon monoxide due to the explosion of H.E. in a confined space. Another was, in fact, chlorine from a sewage chlorination plant that had been hit by H.E. Yet others were harmless oil, found in and around craters. Powders ranging from flour and distemper to Bob Martin's Dog Powders have been reported. The only ones which probably had a hostile origin were such as unburned charges or ashes from parachute flares, dye-bags used to colour the water when airmen had to bale out over the sea or unconsumed H.E. charges. Miscellaneous objects of a suspicious nature occasionally came to a G.I.O. for investigation—" acid bottles " from fire extinguishers; and, in one case, " Molotov bottles " left by military personnel after an exercise.

" Spider Gossamer " caused much excitement in certain districts one autumn, especially as " burns " were reported— which appeared to be due to fragments of nettle entangled in the web.

All these cases might have led to grave alarm in the neighbourhood if they had not been properly handled. Such cases show beyond doubt that G.I.O.'s were to make some useful contribution in the maintenance of public morale and avoidance of undue alarm in many areas and their own morale was sustained by such evidence that their existence was not entirely fruitless.

One further instance might yet be mentioned as clearly indicating the potential value of the service from yet another angle. This did arise in Dagenham. A G.I.O. was undertaking—with the assistance of a small squad of rescue personnel—the disposal of a canister of real mustard gas, opened but not used up during an exercise. Not until this operation was nearing completion was it discovered that one member of the squad was fully convinced it was a " phosphorus bomb " (with which he was acquainted) that was being dealt with, and not the far more dangerous gas.

In early 1944 testing equipment had reached such a high state of development—simplicity with accuracy—that it was possible to distribute new small " pocket testing outfits " among Wardens for their own use on incidents, and the Dagenham G.I.O.'s undertook the training and exercise of 120 Wardens in the use of this new equipment. Also further extension of G.I.O. duties was made, in that it had become clear in paper exercises that a G.I.O. at the side of the Controlling Officer was of great service in assessing the special features of chemical warfare incidents in the Control Room, as well as the G.I.O. in the field.

The Decontamination Service for anti-gas was composed entirely of volunteers. During the early days of the war and before, the services which were trained to deal with gas were very much to the fore, and the training was intense. It called for great care and attention to detail, and for a high standard of physical fitness to endure the conditions consequent upon working in anti-gas clothing.

This Service, fortunately, was not called upon to function as a Decontamination Service but its members (all Council employees) served in a dual capacity, and were used on road damage and repairs. The early days brought long periods of training and preparation and later involved not only decontamination of roads but also food, with which Service they were eventually joined on a basis of interchange.

The equipment which had to be held in readiness was always kept up to standard, and in addition, huge stores of bleaching powder were held in the Borough. As the technical knowledge of the Government increased so the methods of dealing with gas were altered. This fact alone caused training to be continued and brought up to date at regular intervals. In operations the Decontamination Service would have to work in very close co-operation with all other Services, and it was realised that other Services must also be trained in Decontamination work. This involved the training of the Rescue Service in order that they could assist or carry out the work if the Decontamination parties were not available. The whole training had to budget for the worst and hope for the best.

It was a service organised on very extensive lines with three large decontamination centres complete with shower baths. It involved the destruction of contaminated clothing and the re-clothing of those affected by gas. The emphasis on anti-gas precautions in the Civil Defence Scheme was in the beginning very insistent.

There remains one small but important service, the Road Repair Service. It never occupied the limelight but it was an indispensable job of work.

Highways Repair Squad

Immediately prior to the outbreak of war, volunteers for this service were called for from the employees of the Highways and Works Department, and 12 squads each numbering six men were formed. Plant, tools and transport were arranged together with sleeping facilities and the men stood by from 8 p.m. each night at Valence Depot. The first duty was performed on the 1st September, 1939, and this organisation remained in operation until the 14th September after which date the squads were reduced to three in number. This arrangement went on until the 9th October when it was decided in view of the fact that no enemy action had occurred to modify the scheme, and they remained on call at home.

This organisation was adhered to until May 29th, 1944, when new arrangements were made of one squad complete with transport to report for duty at Valence House each night. The Council employees of all Council Services were enrolled in this scheme, and a rota of 12 squads formed, each squad taking its turn of duty during closed hours so that enemy incidents was immediately covered during the day or night; the squads came under the instruction of the Highways and Works Superintendent who was responsible to the Borough Engineer for the clearing of debris from roads and repairs of roads and sewers following bomb damage. They were engaged in this work only at night and during week ends, the main work of repairs being carried out by the Highways and Works staff in the usual manner. The work entailed the clearing of debris on highways with the object of making clearance for traffic at the earliest possible moment and the first aid attention to damaged roads and sewers and generally preparing the work in readiness for the Council's repair gangs to take over at starting times.

Much valuable work was done in this direction notably at the incident at New Road by the " Angler's Retreat " where this heavily trafficked road was completely blocked partly by a large crater and partly by debris.   In co-operation with the Civil Defence Rescue Squads the road was opened to single line traffic in a few hours.   Unofficial thanks were received from High Quarters for the expediency with which this work was carried out in order to clear the road for very considerable military traffic.

The maintenance of full passage for traffic was the primary object of these squads and they proved a valuable asset.

CHAPTER THREE
MEDICAL SERVICES

THE medical services within the Borough were based on a two-tier organisation. The hospital services were in the hands of the Ministry of Health who set up emergency hospitals in dangerous areas for the immediate treatment of casualties, including surgery, etc. Also, certain hospitals (out of London) were organised for specialist attention—head injuries in one place, limb injuries in another. Face injuries, including plastic surgery, were dealt with in another hospital, and so on.

The bottom tier of this organisation was the Borough medical services intended to deal with the air raid casualties on the site of the incident or in the First Aid Post. They covered three sections—casualty service, ambulance service, and the maintenance of the Mortuary.

The Casualty Services were organised in five first aid posts (later reduced to four, and in January, 1945 to three) which were manned by trained nursing staff day and night. In addition, a mobile first aid unit consisting of a travelling medical unit with doctor and nurses, was maintained for the first part of the war but discarded later in favour of two light mobile units.

The organisation of the casualty services commenced in September, 1938. Medical supplies and equipment were purchased. One hundred and ninety-six volunteers manned the first aid posts and ambulances. This hastily assembled organisation was capable of work if war had broken out. Munich, however, saw an end to these preparations, but immediately an extensive programme of recruitment and training was commenced. In November, St. John Ambulance lectures were commenced for volunteers who had already passed an anti-gas course. (Anti-gas treatment was part of the medical services, although not entirely. Anti-gas methods will be dealt with in a separate section.) In the December of 1938 the complete casualty service scheme was placed before the Council, including the erection of first aid posts specially designed and the use of trailer ambulances for towing behind other vehicles. These two aspects of the scheme were not approved by the Essex County Council but the training of volunteers went on energetically. By February of 1939 two hundred and thirty were enrolled out of which one hundred and seven were fully trained. By May all fixed first aid posts and the mobile unit had doctors appointed to them. First aid exercises were held every fortnight. The service was now taking shape and by June five hundred and eighty-three volunteers were enrolled of which number two hundred and thirty-three were fully trained. Training had also been arranged at local factories, and the full-time public health staff—health visitors and sanitary inspectors—had been allocated to first aid posts.

On the day war broke out all five first aid posts were fully manned. The office at the Civic Centre was open day and night for enrolments and first aid lectures were delivered daily, including Sunday. Six days later the mobile unit was equipped and manned, ready for first aid anywhere—it was stationed at the Civic Centre for direction to an incident by Central Control. By the end of September the first aid posts had a full establishment of women, although male staff was below requirement. Apart from surgical instruments, all first aid posts were fully equipped with medical supplies.

The staff engaged for this work varied as war requirements changed. The largest number at one time was three hundred and fifty-nine men and women, not counting the permanent staff who carried out supervising duties.

The following table of staff is not without interest :—

		Establishment	Strength
2/1/41	Stretcher Parties .	230 males	186 males
	Fixed F. A. Posts	17 males	17 males
		83 females	81 females
	Mobile F. A. Posts	18 females	18 females
	Ambulance and Cars	60 males	18 males
		121 females	108 females
3/1/42	Stretcher Parties .	240 males	200 males
	Fixed F. A. Posts	17 males	16 males
		83 females	84 females
	Mobile F. A. Post	2 males	2 males
		18 females	16 females

		Establishment	Strength
31/12/42	Fixed F. A. Posts	8 males 34 females	8 males 32 females
	Mobile F. A. Post	8 females	9 females
	Ambulances and Cars	102 males and females	15 males 74 females
31/12/43	Fixed F. A. Posts	8 males 34 females	6 males 33 females
	Mobile F. A. Post	8 females	7 females
	Ambulances and Cars	70 males and females	11 males 65 females
12/5/45	Fixed F. A. Posts	24 males and females	5 males 19 females
	Mobile F. A. Post	8 females	7 females
	Ambulances and Cars	46 males and females	8 males 36 females

This was a large organisation, capable, and trained for a large number of casualties. Fortunately, casualties to great numbers did not occur.

Total casualties of all kinds amounted to one thousand eight hundred and seventy. These were treated as follows :—

Sent to hospital		584
At first aid posts :—		
Chadwell Heath . . .	195	
Becontree Avenue . . .	114	
Five Elms	433	
Ford Road	296	
Rush Green	7	
Mobile Units	51	
	——	1,096
Fatal casualties		190
		1,870

There is some small discrepancy between casualties reported to Control and the numbers treated at first aid posts but this is possibly accounted for by casualties of a slight character.

The Chadwell Heath First Aid Post (then in part of Whalebone School) was destroyed by a mine at the beginning of 1941. There were no casualties among the staff, although a large school was entirely destroyed. A specially built first aid post was eventually opened in 1943, after enduring a not very comfortable existence in the old Chadwell Heath Infants' School.

The ambulance service consisted of eleven sitting case cars, twenty-six ambulances (later reduced) with a staff of over one hundred at one period, and was controlled as part of the medical service. There was also a special ambulance organisation for the evacuation of hospitals in the case of heavy bombing. This was not put into operation except where the Ministry of Health emptied a number of London hospitals during the fly bomb period.

Such organised movements of serious casualties were not the affair of the Borough Council. Although the Rush Green Hospital is governed by a joint body from three authorities, one of which is Dagenham, the Ministry were responsible for its administration as an emergency hospital. Hospital cases were sent there or to Oldchurch or to King George Hospital, Ilford. These three hospitals upheld the highest hospital traditions throughout the war and each one of them had at least one direct hit by bombs and many near misses.

A mortuary (inevitable provision) was arranged in the old school at Beacontree Heath. Every attempt was made to provide decently for the reception of fatal casualties and for the identification by next of kin.

The first casualty to be received was a Ford worker killed by an oil bomb on 18th September, 1940. (He was cycling alone—the only person on the long approach to the factory. He was killed outright.) The first blitz provided the largest number of casualties, including a naval squad and a squad of bomb removal soldiers. Eventually, after a good deal of discussion with the Education Authorities, the Mortuary was moved to a fresh home but fortunately its purpose was not further required.

Part of this service was the provision of civilian burials. Assistance was provided for those who wished it and every effort made to conduct these interments in a decent Christian tradition.

One important detail of anti-gas services was conducted by the Public Health Department and this was the decontamination of foodstuffs affected by poison gas. Every citizen is aware of the emphasis placed by the Government on the enemy's possible use of poison gas, and the training of voluntary personnel to deal with contaminated food continued throughout the period. Demonstrations and lectures were regularly arranged and attended. As the war progressed, the original volunteers departed into the Services and new volunteers were found. These eventually were drawn from the staffs of the larger retail stores in the Borough.

The airing and decontamination sheds (don't confuse these with those brick buildings intended for contaminated human beings) were built and used regularly for demonstration. A full-scale exercise, in conjunction with the gas decontamination service (full-time, this was), was cancelled as it fell on " D " Day.

The reader will appreciate the effort and difficulty in maintaining interest in a danger that seemed a somewhat remote possibility. It was a question of everybody walking in step despite private doubts about its use. A cautionary measure but work all the same.

CHAPTER FOUR
EVACUATION

EVACUATION was part and parcel of the general scheme of Civil Defence. The first Air Raid Precaution Act of December, 1937, made no provision for evacuation. The Civil Defence Act of 1939 (2 and 3 George 6 C.31) enlarged the whole scope of Civil Defence and in Part 7 (Miscellaneous) Section 56, authority is given for the transference of the Civil population from one area to another in the event of war, or the imminence of war.

As a result of this Act the country was divided into evacuation, reception and neutral areas. When the general evacuation scheme was announced by the Minister of Health, Dagenham was listed as a neutral area. A protest was addressed to the Ministry on the 11th January, 1939, and a deputation consisting of the Mayor, Aldermen and Officers was received at the Ministry on the 31st January, 1939. They presented an impressive memorial of local feeling on the subject. On the 13th June following, the Ministry of Health informed the Borough Council that Dagenham was now an evacuable area—under the term of the 1939 Act. This was Evacuation Plan 3. Plan 2 (the smaller number of areas plan) was superseded; what the Plan 1 was is not known. The date is worth noting because eight weeks later the scheme was put into operation.

By the middle of August, 1939, plans and arrangements for London were practically completed. The local situation in Dagenham was very uncertain, the Ministry were doubtful of operating Plan 3 owing to billeting difficulties. The operation of Plan 2 would have excluded Dagenham. The uncertainty about Plan 3 was cleared by a suggestion from the Directors of the General Steam Navigation Company who suggested to the Ministry the transport of evacuees from the Riverside boroughs to coastal ports in their boats. The suggestion was adopted and on the Monday of the week in which evacuation was carried out the scheme was announced and registration for evacuation commenced. The registration of school children and the make up of their parties was carried out entirely by the schools and this great contribution to the preparation was the work of the Dagenham school teachers. Registration of mothers and children was carried out at the Civic Centre.

It was not a simple task to carry out the scheme. All that part of London included in Plan 2 had had a year's preparation and a full dress rehearsal of school evacuation. For us in Dagenham it was a terrific stretch of work on improvised lines. Almost the entire Council's staff (apart from those organising A.R.P.) was eventually involved. The schools completed their rolls, enlisted their own helpers and banded themselves into well organised groups, led by head teachers and their assistants. It was not so easy to organise the large parties of mothers travelling with their children at such short notice.

In broad outline the plan was that parties of school children with teachers and helpers and parties of mothers with their children would assemble at an assigned school. The Ford Motor Company offered the use of their loading jetties for embarkation and the G.S.N. boats would tie up for embarkation. We were advised that the following boats would be available :—

" Royal Eagle "
" Crested Eagle "
" Golden Eagle "
" Royal Sovereign "
" Queen Charlotte "
" Medway Queen "
" City of Rochester "

The total loading capacity for one sailing was 11,902. I remember plainly that the " Laguna Belle " was eventually included among the boats. I mention this because this was the first time these boats went out on war work—some of them have been lost on active service and the " Laguna Belle " is alleged to have been lost at Dunkirk. A recent press report named the " Golden Eagle " as an " ack-ack " boat. Each boat was assigned a destination at Lowestoft, Yarmouth or Felixstowe.

On Thursday, 27th August, instructions were received to proceed with the evacuation of the Borough. The boats plying on their accustomed holiday trips were recalled by wireless, one as she entered Ostend harbour.   They berthed on Thursday evening off the Ford jetties for two days' work on evacuation.   In the very early hours of the Friday morning, mothers and children formed the first day's parties at their assigned schools and moved off in orderly parties for the long walk to the river.

The southern part of the Borough was assumed to be the most dangerous zone (how wrong we turned out to be), and they were assigned the first embarkation.   It was a lovely sunrise and the last boat slipped her moorings soon after eight o'clock into the golden haze of the river.   One personal impression—an awful silence.   The children did not sing. A return to work for the next day's sailings to find an urgent message from the Ministry to the effect that evacuees must not exceed a total of 20,292 because otherwise there would be no billets for them.   We were greatly comforted by this message—all would be well.   Final loadings were completed on the Saturday morning, a day of drenching pouring rain and unrelieved gloom, with a *two-by-two* procession reminiscent of *another* embarkation in equally wet weather.   The following figures were those registered for evacuation :—

School children (with 666 teachers and 266 helpers)	7,248
Mothers and children	8,514
Expectant mothers ˙	290
Total registration	16,894

Many changed their minds even on the point of embarkation ;   others appeared who were not registered.   An exact tally was impossible to take owing to numbers and the need for leaving the Ford jetties before the day's work commenced at the factory.   Arrangements for their reception at Yarmouth, Lowestoft and Felixstowe were in the hands of the Ministry and local reception officials—plans were not made known to us.   We felt confident about arrangements for their welfare. On Monday, 3rd September, evacuees began to return. Various stories were related and it was decided to send a deputation to Suffolk and Norfolk at once.   Investigations were started in Suffolk on September 6th.   Their report is interesting reading : it *was* true that mothers and children slept on straw for three nights, could not get adequate food and that great distress was suffered by this class of evacuee. Greater numbers had arrived than were expected. At Lowestoft, the Army commandeered all transport intended to convey evacuees into the rural areas behind the coast— this happened and that happened. The deputation found the rural authorities concerned, 26 in number, and found that school children in charge of teachers had settled down pretty well. Mothers with their children were without leaders and many in distress. The deputation stated that on the whole the evacuees were met with great humanity and goodness of heart. We learnt the location of our parties in the rural areas behind the coast. One cannot over-emphasise the work of the school teachers in this scheme. Some of them for several days cooked meals for whole schools of children in temporary communal billets, they guarded their billeting arrangements, sought clothes for them and showed a devotion to duty that few people knew about or realised. Their personal lives had suffered a break up equal to the evacuees but the six hundred odd teachers that went out with the children saved the scheme from foundering entirely.

The report of the deputation made it clear that mothers with their children needed help and guidance urgently. The school children were well looked after by their teachers. An officer was detailed to work in the Reception Areas at once accompanied by a lady member of the Council. There they worked over the two counties for six months, devoting time to visiting all school parties, finding evacuated mothers and giving them assistance, reporting on difficulties, and suggesting monetary aid where needed. Altogether, they covered some thousands of miles. One result of their work was the question of clothing, and the need for immediate assistance for the school children. Local funds and working parties had been got up immediately in the reception areas but more substantial assistance was needed.

The Dagenham Welfare Evacuation Committee (the Mayor and lady councillors) was set up. A fund for clothing children was opened by the middle of October, 1939, which received great support, and subscriptions to the value of nearly £1,000 were received before the Government clothing scheme came into operation under the L.C.C. and this work was no longer wanted. Grants of money, materials and clothing went out rapidly to the reception areas and tided over a difficult initial settling period. Working parties were set up all over the Borough and in schools—clothes went out in good numbers.

From the minutes it can be seen that between September and December, 1939, every endeavour was made to settle unforeseen problems. A number of questions were asked in Parliament about such things as public assistance in reception areas and working of Assistance Boards. The Ministry were constantly reminded of the need for continued evacuation. A regular unofficial trickle joined the school parties and in November we were allowed to dispatch a complementary party of 375 children to join their school parties in Suffolk and Norfolk. Billets were found by direct contact, as we were still acting independently of the London scheme. A new party was settled at Walsingham (place of pilgrimage).

Eventually, on December 18th of this same year, a deputation was received by the Ministry of Health in which many evacuation troubles were aired, and a sanction obtained to apply £300 of Government Funds to clothing.

The first Christmas of the war arrived. £900 voted from the rates for school parties. The Mayor and Mayoress and a Councillor spent Christmas with the children. Snow and ice everywhere—a car accident—but all went well for the very substantial number of children away. After the Christmas of 1939 the quiet continued, no enemy air activity and a general tendency to think about coming home. The announcement of parents' contributions towards billeting in the previous October had upset many family budgets. The Treasury failed to realise that the weekly rent is the largest fixed item in working-class economy. Children or no children, this went on. The schools had been reopened, like the theatres. London was suffering the doldrums of the phoney war.

Physically and mentally defective children, aged, blind and infirm evacuees had been got away in the meantime, and a new scheme for expectant mothers going to temporary country hospitals was well on its feet. Cheap travel vouchers for parents were introduced in November. One singular piece of work was the organisation by the W.V.S. of

Residential Nurseries for children between 2 and 5 years of age. This had a high record of success. Later the London County Council provided short stay nurseries for young children during the mother's confinement.

The Spring of 1940 was the beginning of a campaign for further organised evacuation on a large scale. " Intelligence " had possibly told the Government when to expect air raiding. On March 16th a leaflet and registration forms were pushed into every door by the Post Office urging parents to send school children away. Very few registration forms were received. Local propaganda added to this and some forty parents' meetings were addressed by members of the Council. Events in Europe finally put a spurt into registration. Germany began her invasion of France and parents commenced to register their children. It was not intended to attempt the evacuation of mothers with children this time. That, with a few exceptions, had not proved a success. Many journeys were made to assigned reception areas for conferences between evacuation and reception authorities. Finally, Plan 4 was put into operation.

Between June 13th and 18th (days of capitulation by the French Army), 4,800 school children with teachers departed to destinations—many in the West Country. Registrations exceeded allotted train space and a subsequent party of school children departed to the rural district of St. Germans in Cornwall.

Immediately after this move another evacuation took place, from the beaches of Dunkirk. A long belt of the East Coast (ten miles wide from the coast) was on this account cleared of the original 1939 evacuees, who went to Warwickshire, Staffordshire and Wales.

By this time everybody had experience in evacuation and all went smoothly. It should not be forgotten—whilst the subject is in mind—the contribution of the reception areas to the scheme. Temporary schools, conversion of premises, drafting of teachers, innumerable problems of this kind. But the greatest task was settling town bred women and children into rural life and rural standards of housing.

However, to return to Plan 4. All went well and a pretty good percentage of children left London. None too soon either, because in no time the first blitz opened and real trouble started. Difficulties arose at once—there was no provision for mothers with their families. In June of 1940, a Ministry of Health memorandum E.V.10 permitted the departure of mothers with children *under five only* if they had a home to go to. Our first families rendered homeless by enemy action had no refuge and many went off to a friendly billeting officer with a hastily scribbled note—no time for typing letters. However, official provision was soon available. Plan 5 evacuation for school children and Plan 7 for families was announced. The latter was first limited to those suffering from enemy action but later enlarged to include all mothers and children. Plan 5 started on 19th September, 1940, and Plan 7 on 7th October. Parties left daily during the blitz and continued at longer intervals until mid-1941.

In October of 1940 Circular 2170 (greatest of boons) permitted evacuees to go to any home they had in a reception area. This was an inspired circular and permitted evacuees to go to any home they had in a reception area. The bulk of " fly bomb " evacuation was conducted under its provisions. Circular 2249 (December, 1940) for unaccompanied children allowed similar facilities for children without mothers. I observe in a report dated 23rd July, 1941 that this move out involved 15,000 evacuees, despite Plan 4 carried out before the blitz. Two-thirds of these went under the provision of Circular 2170. I notice quite a number went to Eire and among the evacuees were infants going to nurseries, aged going to hostels, and physically and mentally defective children going to special camps organised by the L.C.C. The organised parties spread over most of England, Derbyshire, to Cornwall. By the Christmas of 1940 only one child in six remained in London.

By the middle of 1941 air raiding was only sporadic. Recollections were still vivid of the great fire raid of 10th May, but May saw the last routine raid. In July, 1941, compulsory evacuation powers were introduced but used only very rarely. The Christmas of 1941 (third of the war) went past with festivities for children away and visits from members of the

Council. Every effort was made to ease the position in the country and keep parties settled down, but we had a long quiet spell, not often broken by gunfire or bombs. Numbers away dwindled and although great events were being enacted abroad, the home front from a war point of view was quiet. It is just a year ago since that quiet was broken. " D " Day, a day for ever sharper in the memory than " VE " Day came, and the almost last answer—the flying bomb.

It is hardly necessary to recall days that are so fresh in recollection. Evacuation became at once an urgent duty in common with all Civil Defence measures. 16,723 evacuees left Dagenham between July 5th and August 31st. Of this number only 5,603 went to homes under the official scheme. The remainder, under Circular 2170, were assisted to homes found by the intending evacuees and provided with billeting allowances. It was a larger exodus than that of 1939. By the end of August, 1944, it is reasonable to assume that 20,000 people, or almost one-quarter of the population were away. I recollect very plainly one incident of this large movement of people. I was standing on a naked unprotected railway platform with several hundred children when a warning sounded. There was no nearby shelter for such a number. The approach of a flying bomb was heard. It passed directly overhead at a very low altitude. Except for a complete silence not one child showed the slightest sign of fright or panic. An unpleasant moment for those in charge of them.

The announcement that " The battle of the flying bomb is won " was the signal for a return home almost unprecedented in the history of railway travel. Evacuation facilities were cancelled during September although those still away received the usual allowances. The " flying gas main " arrived; not very noticeably at first but in increasing numbers. Many regretted their return journey. The Government were asked to restore evacuation facilities and a simultaneous request from East London authorities instigated by Dagenham, restored facilities for those who had a home to go to. The numbers who went away were small. We all got used to it— at last it was quiet, except when the silently falling meteor touched ground.

. Throughout the war 52,000 evacuees had left and returned and left Dagenham again. Between the ending of the fly bomb period and the following Christmas, the vast bulk of Londoners returned home. When the final count for the return home was made, the total number of Dagenham evacuees left in reception areas was under 2,000. A singularly high proportion of these were aged people. The warm and natural instinct for home was too ardent for the slow official arrangements for return (made by the Ministry) and there was no victorious home-coming—each made his own way quickly—home.

Interior of Ford's Motor Company works following a bombing raid. 1939 - 1945

LBBD Archives at Valence House (DS914)

Unknown road in Barking and Dagenham after it had been hit during a bombing raid. 1939 - 1945

CHAPTER FIVE

ASSISTANCE FOR CIVILIANS; BILLETING, REHOUSING, REST CENTRES, INFORMATION

ONE urgent human problem brought to the surface by enemy action was billeting and rehousing the homeless.

Soon after the war started, the Mayor was instructed to appoint Billeting Officers for the various Wards of the Borough in an honorary capacity, the following Council members being asked to accept the appointments :—

Chief Billeting Officer—Alderman F. G. Thomas.
Billeting Officers—Aldermen R. J. D. Clack and W. F.
      Legon.
      Councillors F. Grindrod, M. Reddy,
      C. Thorneycroft and S. Deeks.

It was thought that in billeting strangers on a local household they could inspire confidence.

The first experience of billeting can be now met with a smile. The Borough was warned to prepare to receive Belgian refugees (what a period in the war !—the ninepins falling all over Europe). The older generation remembered well enough another generation of Belgian refugees and plans were made accordingly. But only a few women and children arrived with pathetic bundles, the majority were large well-dressed and well-fed gentlemen, one hundred and seventy-three of them, who were part of the Belgian Civil Service. When the Belgian Government left Brussels they got to the coast to embark (it was thought) for another seat of government, but they only arrived at an English port as evacuees pure and simple. Their luggage alone was a major problem of transport and every available car mustered for carrying it. They did not stay long, as they were gradually absorbed by the Belgian Government, but they seemed to like it and addressed grateful letters to " Ma chére maman."

The first onslaught of the blitz on September 7th, 1940, hit the old East End of London a terrific blow, and for one brief moment, the East-Enders were caught out on one foot. They fled in very considerable numbers to the eastern fringe of London—to the places where they had spent summer Sundays in warm weather, Epping Forest and round about. The East End authorities were overwhelmed by their problem of billeting the homeless and a school full of homeless had a dreadful direct hit right at the beginning. Large numbers were brought to the outer areas, six hundred of them being brought to Chadwell Heath. They lived in the Baptist Hall, which eventually housed a total of 2,570 evacuees during September and October. This was not all, because many Dagenham people had parents and relations in the eastern boroughs who came out to them in very large numbers—ten thousand in a week at the first onset.

This one aspect of billeting demanded a much larger organisation than was at first envisaged, and full-time Billeting Officer became necessary. Mr. Thomas was asked to carry on in this position, which he continued until 1942.

That was only one side of the work. The other was the temporary housing of those whose homes were damaged but capable of repair.

Some sort of plan was made in the first place by the Essex County Council's Public Assistance Department. A land-mine (the first one) on Rylands Estate on 17th September, 1940, put this provision to the test, with the result that the Borough Council felt that new and improved arrangements had to be made at once.

The Billeting Officer and the Borough Treasurer were requested by the Emergency Committee of the Council to prepare a scheme for Rest Centres, to cover the whole of the Borough, as quickly as possible. A plan was quickly submitted and the necessary permission obtained from the various departments at County Hall, Chelmsford. The first Rest Centre under the control of the Borough Council was opened on 7th October, 1940 at Halbutt School. It was run by Mrs. Legon and a band of voluntary helpers and they kept a twenty-four hour service going throughout the war.

Other Rest Centres were opened at Lymington School and at the Scouts Hall, Chadwell Heath. Stand-by Rest Centres were also arranged at various schools throughout the district, all ready to be manned at a moment's notice by voluntary helpers.

To give a brief summary, the following figures will indicate the task which had to be undertaken :—

Persons who stayed at Rest Centres owing to loss of homes (temporary or otherwise) . .	9,170
Number of bombed-out people officially billeted	13,456
Number of persons rehoused in requisitioned properties from August, 1940 to November, 1946	1,396
Numbers rendered temporarily homeless by piloted aircraft from August, 1940 to June, 1944	7,905
Numbers rendered temporarily homeless by " V " weapon attacks from June, 1944 onwards .	1,265
Enrolled voluntary helpers	120

The Rehousing Department also sold official Ministry furniture to those who had lost their homes, and much assistance was given in housing war workers, also, by loaning bedding and other essentials. When the war was over, the Department assisted in the same manner with the return of evacuated children.

This is one Department which has not closed down—it has been merged into the Housing Department and is deeply engaged in post-war housing.

The bare recital of these facts does not convey all that these " Cinderella " jobs meant. The Rest Centre service was under the same leader all during the war and much of the work—meals for hundreds at a time—done by voluntary labour.

It was work always done under air raid conditions, and much of it in the very dark hours. Children were looked after whilst parents went to straighten out their collapsed homes as best they could. They were kind and informal sort of places, cheerful, helpful and good tempered. On one occasion a wedding party was given a riotous send off from a

Rest Centre, and they were more than once the scenes of seasonal celebrations.

The Information Centre (not the Ministry of Information) was set up to give help and advice to people who had suffered and sustained damage to their homes through enemy air attacks. The main feature of the scheme was that these people could receive this aid in one building, and when the necessity arose, the Food Office, Evacuation Department and Assistance Board had representatives in the Civic Centre with the Departments of the Corporation concerned with bombed out people.

It was first brought into operation in 1941, following experience gained in the 1940/1941 blitz, and from then until the intensification of enemy air attack in 1944, the Centre gave valuable and extensive advice to persons who had been injured or had lost property.

From February, 1944 until March, 1945, the date of the last rocket incident in Dagenham, nearly 6,000 people were interviewed. Quite a number of these had lost everything— homes, furniture, food, clothes, and in some cases, one or more of their family. To all, the Information Centre gave advice concerning emergency arrangements for billeting, housing, clothing, claims, etc. From there they were directed, according to their needs, to the appropriate rooms in the Civic Centre for—

> money and clothing for their immediate requirements from the Assistance Board ;
>
> billeting, rehousing and furniture from the Rehousing Officer ;
>
> emergency ration cards from the Ministry of Food representative ;
>
> removal and storage of furniture and information upon repair of war damage from the Borough Surveyor's Department ;
>
> evacuation arrangements from the Evacuation Officer.

Information was also given to relatives and friends concerning the whereabouts of injured persons.

For two or three days following a serious incident, large numbers of residents came to the Information Centre for assistance and advice. In order to cope with these numbers the hall outside the entrance to the Council Chamber was turned into a waiting room, with seating capacity for nearly 150 people, and tea was supplied, free of charge, throughout the day.

To save travelling, arrangements were made to set up the Information Centre temporarily in the vicinity of serious incidents should it be warranted. This scheme was operated three times in respect of incidents in the Chadwell Heath area when the Information Centre was set up at the Branch Library, Warren Schools and the Chadwell Heath Nursery.

Many questions were answered and, in addition, the Information Centre (with the aid of the Branch Libraries) supplied soap for cleansing purposes. Since the cessation of enemy air attack and the speeding up of war damage repairs, many hundredweights of soap have been sold to help residents to clean their homes after completion of the repairs.

The work of the Information Centre still goes on, and many residents, particularly those who have returned from evacuation, or service in the Forces, are now seeking advice about the position of their war damage claims, etc. Where the claims are still unsettled, advice is given as to how and where they can obtain settlement, or at least part of their claim, if they are in need of money to help in rehabilitating themselves after some years of makeshift following the loss of their homes.

The Ministry of Information Local Committee was formed in 1941 (in face of the invasion threat) by the Mayor at the request of the Minister of Information. It comprised members of the Council and representatives of political parties, Chambers of Trade, press, teachers, organised labour, etc.

Its main object was to be a channel of information and support the local " morale." It was originally intended to be an agency for dispelling rumours but the unwillingness or inability of Central Department to issue the facts connected with matters of public discussion almost entirely defeated this object.

Notwithstanding the shadow under which the Ministry itself existed for a large part of its career, the Committee performed some useful, if unspectacular work in the realm of film shows, talks, exhibitions and intelligence reports (containing public reactions) on various aspects of the war effort and preparing the public for new phases of the war.

The severity of the Coventry air raid and the inadequate provision made to meet the local public needs for information on numerous matters, did not pass unnoticed. And with the comparative lull in bombing in 1942/43, the organisation to deal with emergencies was reviewed. This resulted in the appointment of an Emergency Information Officer in the most vulnerable areas. His duties were twofold—

(a) to be the channel for official communications to the public in the event of invasion by the enemy ;

(b) to disseminate essential information concerning the working of public services after severe enemy attack.

His media were to be bulletin boards and a network of subsidiary information officers organised on the Civil Defence sectors, wireless loudspeaker vans, posters, special editions of newspapers, etc.

The paper scheme was completed and exercises took place, but there was little real call on the organisation—fortunately no subsequent misfortune at the hands of the enemy was on a sufficient scale seriously to disrupt the local public services.

The W.V.S. later took over the dissemination of *immediate* after-raid information and tribute must be paid to the rapidity with which they manned information points—often in a derelict shop without windows or some hopelessly inadequate shelter in the near vicinity of the incident.

The Town Clerk had custody of valuables retrieved from the wrecked homes by the Civil Defence Services.

Every endeavour was made to trace the owners of valuables which were found on the bombed sites. The Department handled hundreds of pounds in cash, bonds and Savings Certificates ; jewellery, watches and insurance policies, were also much in evidence amongst salvaged goods.

CHAPTER SIX

FOOD SERVICES

BRITISH Restaurants became a common sight on the war-time landscape towards the end of 1940. They played a double part in providing cheap meals cooked on a large communal basis economising fuel and heat. That was the obvious use. The second was to provide the foundation of a national emergency feeding organisation should this become necessary. The war never got as bad as that for England, but it is probably not generally known that had there been a complete breakdown in the standard ways of life, caused perhaps by invasion, there existed an organisation capable of feeding the entire civilian population. Iron rations were kept in storage, and frequently changed, all over the country. Had the war taken a different course, no one would have starved.

The British Restaurants were an important part of this plan. Their kitchens and dining rooms, always in use, provided a good foundation for community feeding centres.

The local restaurants were started in the early part of 1940. St. George's Restaurant, in the road of that name, was followed quickly by Goresbrook. In March, 1942 the tea room at the Mayfair Cinema was converted into a third restaurant. No further suitable buildings were available so prefabricated restaurants were built in Chadwell Heath and by the eastern factory area at Four Wantz. The latter is a very large canteen capable of seating five hundred people for a meal at one time.

British Restaurants did more than serve meals in their dining rooms. Meals were carried in heated containers to small factories and works who had no canteens such as Crollies, Hippersons, etc. Bomb repair workers were fed entirely by them.

The following figures are interesting in their significance :—

Number of meals served in 1943/44 . . 749,719
,,   ,,   ,, 1944/45 . . 585,467
,,   ,,   ,, 1945/46 . . 489,986

Originally, all meals supplied to Dagenham schoolchildren came from British Restaurants and this reached a peak about April, 1944, when 11,000 meals were supplied for the month. After this time the Essex County Council gradually established kitchens at their schools and dealt with the feeding themselves. The number of meals supplied to schools in April, 1945 had fallen to 3,000.

The following figures show the number of meals supplied and the weekly average for the last 2½ years :—

	Gores-brook	Mayfair	St. Chads	St. Georges	Wantz	Total
1943/44						
Total Meals	240,161	55,324	97,744	241,262	*115,228	749,719
weekly average	4,618	1,064	1,880	4,640	4,268	16,470
1944/45						
Total Meals	169,421	40,080	88,740	156,404	130,822	585,467
weekly average	3,258	771	1,707	3,008	2,516	11,259
1945/46						
Total Meals	138,279	*23,505	76,621	142,809	108,772	489,986
weekly average	2,659	635	1,473	2,746	2,092	9,605

* Open for 8½ months only.

The financial results of the Restaurants have been satisfactory in spite of temporary difficulties.

During the year 1944/5 there was a net loss of £449 after providing £2,257 in repayment of the cost of the assets but omitting any payment for central administrative charges. This loss was largely the result of the flying bombs and rockets which resulted in considerable evacuation of the population and made many who stayed, reluctant to leave their homes.

In 1945/6 a net profit of £1,969 was made and the year 1946/7 shows still more favourable results.

The Council decided that a special rate should be charged in the case of Old Age Pensioners and was originally 6d. per meal inclusive as against 1s. 0d. for the ordinary adult person. The charge to pensioners was increased in January, 1944 to 7d. and again in July, 1945 to 10d. This was necessary as the Undertaking was making a loss and the difference between the prices charged to Old Age Pensioners and those charged to ordinary customers would fall upon the rates. A good deal of miscellaneous feeding was also carried on in Civil Defence canteens and in Parks and Swimming Pools.

The object of the Emergency Feeding Service was to cater for those persons who, whilst not destitute or homeless, were unable to obtain meals from normal sources as a result of enemy action or other similar reasons. In February, 1941 the Ministry of Food requested Local Authorities to establish the service to cater for at least 10 per cent. of the population in addition to Rest Centre provisions.

The service, operated under the auspices of the Ministry, was primarily directed towards the first few days after heavy bombardment. The following salient features had to be incorporated in the arrangements made. The Centres were to be :—

1. As widely dispersed over the area as possible.
2. Sited in the least vulnerable areas.
3. Independent of gas and electricity for cooking purposes.
4. Independent of a piped water supply.
5. Efficiently blacked-out.
6. Equipped with food stocks and certain equipment supplied by the Ministry.

In December it was felt that the area, lying on the outskirts of London, it was likely that in the event of serious attacks on the capital there would be an influx of population from the more central areas. This matter was discussed with the Ministry and the Dagenham provision was raised to cater for 28,000 additional population instead of 10,000.

The following arrangements were then made in Dagenham :—

Twenty centres catering for 1,000 people each and four for 2,000 people were ordered. Each school was equipped with four solid fuel 20 gallon boilers. Twelve schools were equipped with cooking ranges. The cost of this provision was £869, apart from the cost of equipment. Each school was provided with six water casks, each cask holding 150 gallons. The initial provision for this item cost £446 and installing the water barrels on brick platforms an additional £362.

The supply was kept in good condition by a chlorination process and a mobile water tank was also purchased for refilling the barrels and detailed arrangements made with the Water Company for more extensive refilling from local wells.

That part of each school required for Emergency Feeding was scheduled and earmarked by the Ministry to prevent its requisition for any other Government purpose. Each school was provided with black-out for the accommodation reserved. The total cost of black-out was £919.

The Ministry provided the food stocks for the centres. These stocks consisted of tinned milk, soups, margarine, biscuits, rice pudding, meat roll, etc., to a total weight of over 100 tons.

It must be borne in mind that Dagenham was only a part in a very comprehensive scheme. The industrial and other catering establishments were asked to give details of their equipment and output for these establishments to be included in the scheme. In the event of necessity requiring the operation of the scheme the British Restaurants would have immediately become Emergency Feeding Centres, and whilst the industrial and other catering establishments would be fully occupied in catering for the industrial workers in the area, arrangements were made for some of the industrial canteens (e.g. Ford's) to supply meals (mainly during the night) for transportation elsewhere.

The Ford Motor Company had generously provided the Ministry of Food with Emergency Food Vans. Dagenham was allotted two of these which were serviced free of cost by Reynolds Motors, Ltd. These were mainly used by the British Restaurants and for school feeding purposes.

Every assistance was given to the scheme by the Head Teachers of the selected schools, who volunteered to act as Leaders. Members of the Council volunteered their services as Liaison Officers. In all, 660 persons were enrolled as members of the Borough Civil Defence organisation on this service alone.

Mobile Feeding Units consisted of a portable shed with portable cooking apparatus and equipment. Dagenham was allocated three of these units to supplement the static centres. Each unit had an initial allocation of food sufficient to feed 500 people for one week. During the fly bomb period these units were set up at 11 incidents in the Borough and gave valuable assistance, being manned by members of the W.V.S.

CHAPTER SEVEN

FOOD AND FUEL OFFICES

THE Rationing System as we now know it was born in 1938 in order to ensure the equitable feeding of the entire population in event of war. The experience gained during the Great War of 1914–1918 enabled the building up by the Ministry of Food of an organisation to deal with all supplies of foodstuffs from the point of production to the individual consumer. The whole country was divided into divisions, each of which was controlled by a Divisional Food Officer who was responsible to, and under the control of, the Ministry of Food Headquarters. Each division was in turn sub-divided into the units comprising Local Government Boroughs or Areas.

Prior to the war these local authorities were asked to select their Food Executive Officers and key personnel from their staffs and to appoint Local Food Control Committees consisting of representatives of consumers and traders. This composition was designed to enable the Committee to consider and protect the interest of consumers, with the added advantage of having the practical advice of food distributors and traders and their employees.

The Food Executive Officer, appointed by the Divisional Food Officer on behalf of the Ministry of Food, acted as Secretary of the Food Control Committee and was in charge of the Food Office and its staff. Thus, on the outbreak of war in 1939, the framework was ready. The Borough Treasurer (Mr. H. O. W. Bigg) became the first Food Executive Officer, and a number of the Council's staff were there to assist him.

The Committee had also been appointed and was composed of five trade members—a grocer, a butcher, a baker, and a milk distributor—a Co-operative Society representative, a trade member, and twelve members representing the consumers of the Borough.

The functions of the Committee were mainly in an advisory capacity, although they also investigated complaints and suspected offences against the Ministry's Orders, and had the power to prosecute offenders when this was considered necessary.

The first ration books were issued in January, 1940 and they covered the first six months of the year, just over 88,000 books being sent out. The next issue was made in July, when the number was 92,000. Subsequent issues, in round figures, were—91,800 in 1941, 97,000 in 1942, 95,000 in 1943, 94,500 in 1944, 96,000 in 1945. At the commencement only meat was rationed, but shortly after margarine, butter, fats, bacon, sugar, tea, etc., could only be obtained by means of the ration book. Later still, as commodities became more difficult to obtain, the " Points " system was put into operation. The " Personal Points " for sugar, confectionery and chocolate began in July, 1942, allowing eight ounces for each person every four weeks. Arrangements had also been designed to cover tobacco and cigarettes, if necessary, but this extension of the scheme was never put into operation.

The " Milk Supply Scheme " was brought in in October, 1941, to guarantee supplies to certain classes of consumers, such as expectant mothers, children, adolescents, invalids, and certain institutions (schools, etc.). Consumers had to register with one dairyman and could only obtain supplies from him. The supplies to the distributing dairyman were based on the number of their registrations and priorities, so ensuring that all persons had their full entitlement and that there was no surplus that might have been wasted.

The enforcement of the numerous Food Regulations was an important work of the Food Office, entailing numberless enquiries into alleged offences in all classes of shops handling foodstuffs, instituting proceedings or issuing warnings against offenders. On an average of the cases reported about 45 per cent. resulted in prosecution, 40 per cent. by warnings, and the remaining cases were not sufficiently strong for any action to be taken.

Catering, Communal Feeding and Emergency Feeding were other services dealt with by the Food Office. Restaurants, cafes, canteens, etc., all had to be licensed and supplies issued to them in accordance with the number and type of meals and beverages served. Factory canteens, providing for many thousands of meals each day, but with an increased amount of food rations per meal than allowed to restaurants and cafes used by the general public, also entailed a considerable amount of extra work. The returns made by all these need a deal of checking and supervision.

Meals in schools were also provided through the Education authorities to ensure that growing children had an adequate diet. This was of immense benefit to many families whose mothers were employed on work of national importance.

Immediately after heavy damage through enemy action, emergency Food Offices were opened, usually at the nearest Wardens' Post in the area, for the issue of emergency cards to replace food lost. In manning these posts the staff did valiant work in all weathers and often in unpleasant surroundings. Even at week-ends this was done and on several Sundays the staff worked and local shops not affected were opened to supply immediate needs.

Emergency feeding was also operated as near as possible to an incident involving loss or damage to homes or where essential services ceased to operate. This service was put into operation at many places in the Borough within a short time after heavy bombing, and the W.V.S. performed good work in manning these.

The salvaging of foodstuffs in such cases was another of the Food Office responsibilities and their prompt action was the means of saving large quantities from destruction or loss through bad weather or looting. In one case, for example, some £3,000 worth of goods were salved from a badly damaged shop liable to collapse at any moment. The goods were brought out, stacked and covered over, and guarded all night by some of the staff, and when checked next day it was found that a 3d. packet of powder could not be accounted for.

A scheme was also evolved for mutual assistance on the part of retailers to help each other in cases where their business premises were destroyed or so damaged as to prevent their use. This arrangement ensured that the public would be able to obtain their rationed foods without delay and also that the shopkeeper would be able to carry on until he could obtain other premises. This scheme was first put to test in October, 1940, when a grocer in High Road, Chadwell Heath, had his shop put out of action and stock damaged by a parachute mine about 10 p.m. At 9 a.m. the next morning he was able to serve his customers at the premises and from the stock of another grocer by Japan Road. This facility was given him for several months while his shop was put in temporary repair. Subsequently, similar arrangements were operated when and where required, and a tribute is due to all retailers who helped others in similar circumstances.

Another service which was started in July, 1940, was the National Milk Scheme, which provided all children under five years of age, and expectant mothers, with a guaranteed pint of milk per day, at 2d. per pint (instead of 4½d.), or free if the family income was below a certain level.

For babies under twelve months of age, and who did not thrive on liquid milk, National Dried Milk was provided in tins equivalent to seven pints of liquid milk and at a cost of 1s. 2d. or free if entitled to free liquid milk.

In December, 1941, the Welfare Food Scheme (now Welfare Foods Service) was started and provided blackcurrant syrup or purée and cod liver oil free to children up to two years of age, and early in 1942, the blackcurrant products were replaced by Lease-Lend orange juice. The issues were subject to small payment, except those who were entitled to free supplies of milk automatically received orange juice and cod liver oil free. For expectant mothers, vitamin A and D tablets were provided as an alternative to cod liver oil. The scheme was later merged with normal rationing and all children's green ration books (RB2) contained coupons for obtaining orange juice and cod liver oil.

In February, 1941 a Branch Food Office was opened at 129, Church Elm Lane, to serve the needs of the south part of the Borough and to relieve the pressure on the Civic Centre. Soon afterwards, the Methodist Church Hall on Beacontree Heath was opened to deal with the public side of the work.

In April, 1943, the work of the Food Office had so increased that it was necessary to seek more accommodation than was available at the Civic Centre and the present Main Office at 52/56, Whalebone Lane South was opened. The work in connection with National Registration was at the same time incorporated with the work of the Food Office, which was a heavy addition to normal business.

The local Fuel Office is a curious place. Like the Food Office, the inhabitants of that office know very little about Fuel (apart from consumers' experience) but their duty is to administer the various Fuel and Lighting Orders under the instructions of the Ministry of Fuel. It has no Committee comparable with the Food Committee and it deals in a commodity that is of a very bulky nature.

The rationing of solid fuel is not an easy matter. The intention of the whole scheme is a fair share all round. It was anticipated at one time that electricity and gas would also be rationed and every house in the Borough was given a shadow ration. As there are roughly 25,000 houses, this was a huge undertaking, but after each house was allotted its ration of gas, etc., it was decided that the scheme was not necessary. We were fortunately saved the experience of many Continental towns where gas and light were available only at certain times and the black market in solid fuel a luxury only the very rich could afford. This much may be justly claimed—fuel has often been short but it has rarely been non-existent.

Twice the Borough Council went into the coal trade, during particularly severe weather, and sold coal on a cash-and-carry basis. It was always in extremely cold snowy weather and it was a disagreeable experience for customers and the Council coal merchant. It saved many a hearth from the lack of a fire and people lined up on Sunday mornings cheerfully for a limited quantity of coal. Aged and sick people had coal delivered at their doors.

To help the fuel situation further, a wood fuel scheme was put in hand on a local basis. Over 26,000 baskets and 6,000 sacks of wood were supplied but it was financially unsuccessful. The Government abandoned their own wood fuel scheme for a similar reason. The effort was worthwhile, however, and the scheme achieved part of its original purpose.

Briefly, the principal work of the Fuel Office was the alleviation of hardship, the enforcement of the Fuel and Lighting Orders, and a link between local fuel conditions and the Ministry of Fuel and Power. It is the duty of the Fuel Office to report regularly to the Ministry on the amount of fuel available in local yards and so on.

Many hundreds of thousands of enquiries were handled and assistance given where there was a good claim. Forms, I need not say, were countless in number and for some unfathomable reason this office was given the job of handing out forms for Utility Furniture.

Oval Road, Dagenham, Bomb Damage

Ford's Motor Company works exterior following a bombing raid. 1939 - 1945

LBBD Archives at Valence House (SB1635)

CHAPTER EIGHT

A VARIETY OF SERVICES,
WAR-TIME FARMING AND
ALLOTMENTS, SALVAGE
COLLECTION AND BOOK
DRIVES

IN common with all owners
of lands not being used for agricultural purposes, the Borough
Council turned farmers and ploughed up their playing
fields and parks to add to the production of grain and
root crops for the country. Under the same impetus allotments
were greatly increased in number and every encouragement
given to local men *and* women to grow their own vegetables.

There is something of a very personal nature of this contribution towards the war effort—expenses small but work pretty
hard. In some ways it is a pity that the need for land for
housing, and other urgent purposes, will reduce the number of
allotments on sites where they are easily accessible to homes.

Farmer Borough Council to commence with put under
cultivation 132 acres of park lands and other land in possession
of the Council. A great deal of Central Park and its playing
fields went under the plough. The fact that a little later the
military cut an anti-invasion ditch straight through the same
land was only a minor but very natural irritation to Farmer
Borough Council. Bombs here and there made holes in crops,
an occasional fire from incendiaries (enemy or small boy variety)
were incidents of small interest in the job of growing more
food. Wheat, of course, was the most valuable and valued
crop. Wheat, oats and barley altogether yielded 1327 quarters,
which were sold at good market prices. Potatoes and market
garden produce worked a double tide. They provided
absolutely fresh vegetables for war workers using British
Restaurants. 163 tons of potatoes were grown and other

vegetables too numerous to mention. Altogether the value of crops grown in Dagenham parks from 1939 to 1945 yielded the sum of £11,251 11s. 6d. This paid the cost of labour and cultivation, profits going to the relief of the Rates.

1st Oct. to 30th Sept.	Wheat			Barley			Oats			Fodder			Potatoes			Market Garden, etc.		
	£	s.	d.	£	s.	d.	£	s.	d.	£	s.	d.	£	s.	d.	£	s.	d.
1939–40	660	13	1	—			—			139	2	7	20	4	6	246	8	6
1940–41	604	11	11	205	13	10	345	14	0	581	2	5	190	11	8	412	15	2
1941–42	1073	3	8	108	10	0	344	8	9	383	1	7	247	19	11	292	7	7
1942–43	375	13	0	743	1	2	233	4	0	453	10	4	340	15	11	513	5	10
1943–44	191	10	4	128	5	6	25	0	8	152	19	1	261	18	2	274	2	7
1944–45	418	5	6	383	17	6	301	11	6	35	19	2	350	1	9	212	0	4

The total value of these crops was £11,251 11s. 6d.

Allotments increased vastly in number during the war. Many men, and a few women, turned to the soil for relief and quiet. There is something eminently sane and quietening about gardening and the consciousness of doing a little towards the common effort, and a great deal towards the well-being and health of those at home. Seventeen thousand additional war-time allotments were provided by the Borough Council— the sites covering approximately one hundred and nineteen acres. Gardening instruction was provided by lectures and films. Help was given in the purchase of seeds and fertilisers, and at the end of the summer, an annual show for Horticulture, Fur and Feather was arranged. Altogether, about two thousand families had an interest in an allotment and the contribution it made to the family table.

Salvage

The collection of salvage, kitchen waste and books is an odd trio of subjects, but they were, in fact, all carried out by the normal peace-time salvage disposal plant. The collection, sorting and disposal of salvage is a day-to-day operation in Dagenham, whether at peace or war, but during the war, great salvage drives were organised in order to increase the availability of material for the war effort, particularly metals and paper.

Between 1939 and 1945 the following materials were collected and sold :—

	Tons	Amount realised £
Metals, Bottles, Rags, etc.	8,315	17,412
Waste Paper	3,624	19,143
Clinker	2,801	51
Kitchen Waste	3,336	4,826
	18,076	£41,432

These are astonishing figures, particularly if it is realised, that this was done as part and parcel of getting rid of household rubbish, the greater bulk of which is burned and no more is heard of it.

The kitchen waste organisation was carried out in this way. After collection it was cooked and made into animal food called " Tottenham cake." This was a successful substitute for other animal foods and greatly in demand.

Readers will remember the first book drive for books, which was made after Mr. Churchill's return from Africa. It was an appeal made to all the nation and was organised through the local authorities and the post office. The first of these drives was held in April, 1943 and resulted in the collection of 247,220 books. Two hundred thousand of these books were collected by school children and taken to their schools. The part played by the school children in this part of the war effort was a very considerable one. Of this great total of books, amounting to nearly forty-seven tons, the great bulk was sorted out for salvage and sent away to be made into paper. 26,760 volumes, however, were despatched to the troops. Each one contained a message of goodwill from the people of Dagenham. They brought letters of thanks from every front, and the first one to arrive was from one of the Council's own servants situated in some remote place in North Africa.

A later drive did not yield this great figure, neither can it be expected, but, altogether, about forty thousand books were despatched to the troops during the war and a great mass of paper sent off for making into fresh paper. I daresay that many of these books are now lying about in queer, deserted corners of the world. There is no doubt, as the war progressed, that this vitally important need of the serving man was met with an increasing degree of success, and we all know, now that the men have returned, what a contribution it made to their personal lives whilst away.

CHAPTER NINE

THE CITIZENS' SHARE: THE WOMEN'S VOLUNTARY SERVICE, FORCES HOUSE, NATIONAL SAVINGS AND LOCAL WAR CHARITIES

WE all remember the first appearance of the green tweed coats with maroon hats and blouses. A titter was heard here and there, but as the war went on, the Women's Voluntary Service became the most formidable organisation of women's voluntary effort ever known. There was no work in civilian life where they did not help in some way or another, and many died on duty in air raids. That was here in London. In the country they were the main support of the evacuation and billeting scheme, particularly in the welfare and clothing of children and the evacuation of infants.

The first Dagenham W.V.S. Centre was opened at Valence House in August, 1940. An additional centre was arranged at 87, High Road, Chadwell Heath in October, 1942, and the following December the centre moved into new headquarters on Heathway Bridge. A great recruiting drive in August, 1942, raised the membership from 200 to 2,310 and every one of these women had the care and work of a family already in her hands. It is impossible to say all they did, but these were the principal jobs :—

Sewing parties made clothes for evacuees, made black-out curtains for requisitioned houses, altered hundreds of mattress covers for the rest centres and sewed curtains for camps and batteries. They issued wool parcels for service comforts. They distributed baby clothing to Service wives and organised the knitting of baby clothes for children in Europe. They handled the clothing depot for the bombed out and distributed thousands of garments. The rest centres found their volunteers for cooking among the W.V.S. members. When knitting for Russia was asked for, they got down to it and also looked after the Civil Defence workers' woollen comforts.

Canteens were always out at air raid incidents (day and night) and a W.V.S. woman was inside—her shelter a roof of ply wood. They operated the emergency feeding units—a sort of glorified hot potato merchant outfit that cooked meals three times a day on the kerb when air raids had damaged the normal services.

The Housewives Service was a complete " coverage " over the whole Borough. They did the simple humble jobs—food for Home Guard on exercises, taking blind and crippled people to hospitals and children to nursery schools. They even delivered flowers to wives and sweethearts of Servicemen —it was the " say it with flowers " scheme to cheer up the woman left at home.

At each air raid incident they set up an " enquiry point " to offer advice and answer enquiries from next of kin or to give the present whereabouts of those who had lived in the mound of rubble across the way.

They helped both here and in the reception areas with the Government Evacuation Scheme, and they ran the London Clothing Scheme in the reception areas.

In the latter part of 1944 (and it still goes on) the Rehousing Scheme was started. Towns unharmed by enemy action sent their gifts of furniture to an adopted area. Dagenham received furniture from Wales, Lancashire, Nantwich, Northern Ireland and Brentwood. These gifts have helped many families who suffered a total loss of their household goods. This does not sum up all they did—they permeated the fabric of everyday life. I should be able to provide figures for all these things—I cannot because they did not bother to keep them. The Women's Voluntary Service gave a quality of service that counted neither the time nor the place but was always there with two pairs of hands for each member clad in her green tweed coat.

Forces House

" Forces House " was a comparatively late arrival among war-time activities. I suppose it was the air raid lull that gave time for it, but it was a child of the W.V.S., in so far as the founder and organiser of " Forces House " was Alderman

(Mrs.) Evans, then centre organiser for the W.V.S. A shop was leased in New Road—the fitting up took a time. No sooner was it opened than the shop next door was needed, and from then onwards till the end of the war, " full house " was the usual notice because it provided not only meals but beds and recreation rooms. It was staffed entirely by voluntary labour and the organiser herself not only supervised it but lived there and cooked herself the early morning breakfast for the hotel guests. For some men, particularly from the Dominions, it was their only home and they returned time and again and wrote sending photographs when they returned to their own homes. It was hardly a Palm Beach resort—the back windows looked over the Thameside belt of industry working at full pressure. They did not mind it, the quality of " Forces House " outweighed its disadvantages.

The bare figures convey something of the scale of work involved in this voluntary effort. Between the date of opening in February, 1943 and July, 1945, when it closed, 14,284 soldiers slept at " Forces House." The number of meals is not recorded but they were not less than forty thousand. This work, including cooking, cleaning, and the whole boiling, was done by voluntary workers.

The cost of establishing " Forces House " came from local subscriptions, with strong support from the large firms. The Essex County Welfare Organisation provided furnishings, and help came from a multitude of other sources. The charges made for the use of the house were kept at a low figure and funds required a periodical boosting—they never lacked local support.

National Savings

The existence of the National Savings movement in September, 1939 was indeed fortunate and its expansion to meet the needs of a new war was smooth and rapid. Dagenham, like many other towns, had a Local Savings Committee. It met once a year to review its work. This body immediately strengthened its membership. Sub-Committees were formed to organise propaganda and publicity and to encourage saving in industry, schools and streets.

The street savings group is one of the many remarkable manifestations of community enterprise for which the war was responsible. Beginning early in 1940, the street group campaign enlisted thousands of citizens, mostly housewives, as street group secretaries. By September, 1943, when National Savings reached its peak, there were 128,000 street groups in Great Britain. In Dagenham during this same period, 235 street groups were enrolled and many Dagenham people have cause to thank these voluntary workers for nest-eggs which might not otherwise have been accumulated. The very able Street Groups Sub-Committee, first under the Chairmanship of Mr. G. W. Brady, and later under Mr. G. Brewster, did splendid work ; but the results achieved were mainly due to the energy and enthusiasm of its chief organiser, Mrs. C. A. Murphy.

Much enthusiasm was put into National Savings in places of employment and many very fine efforts were sustained throughout the war. The Ford Motor Company was conspicuous in this field, having over 90 per cent. of its employees enrolled as group members, the highest percentage in the country. The total of investments made through industrial groups was well over £2,000,000, a record for which much of the credit must go to a very energetic Industrial Sub-Committee under the Chairmanship of Mr. S. W. Kallend.

School saving, from the monetary aspect, was, naturally, less spectacular, but from the point of view of group member- ship results were very satisfactory and there was a savings group in every school. The distribution of propaganda and publicity material by the school children was only one of the many ways in which schools were always ready to help the Local Committee. As with industry and streets, an effective Sub-Committee under Miss E. Baker did much to facilitate easy co-operation.

Beginning in 1940, the National Savings Committee organised annual Savings Weeks of which the first four were linked in turn to the fighting services and their equipment, and the last—in 1945—to the expression of thanksgiving for victory. These Weeks gave Local Committees a great deal of hard work and plenty of fun and the results obtained were spectacular. Dagenham's record in these events is given at the end of this review. Each week necessitated many weeks of preparation. Processions of service, pre-service and A.R.P. units were organised. Concerts, Whist Drives, and other entertainments provided substantial sums of money which paid the expenses of the Week and also enabled the Local Committee to make donations to service and local charities. Selling Centres at which the public could make their investments were opened in all parts of the Borough.

A very successful idea was introduced into the 1942 " Warships " Week. Local Committees were invited to raise a sum of money which would provide the Navy with a ship and those who did so were permitted by the Admiralty to " adopt " a vessel of the type provided.

In this way Dagenham adopted a recently launched Destroyer of the Hunt Class—H.M.S. " Limbourne," a Comforts Fund was established for her by public subscription and she put to sea with a fine variety of sports equipment and amenities including books and periodicals, theatrical " props," electric irons, wringers, sun-ray lamps, and two bicycles. Bicycles seemed strange items in a ship's equipment until the Commanding Officer explained how useful they were in making for speedier communication between dock and town. Commemoration Plaques were exchanged between the " Limbourne " and the Borough of Dagenham, one being placed on the ship's quarter-deck and the other in the Hall of Dagenham's Civic Centre. In October, 1943 " Limbourne " was sunk in action off the Channel Islands with considerable loss of life. A balance of £303 remaining in the " Limbourne " Comforts Fund was sent to the Royal Naval Benevolent Trust to be used for any survivors or dependents who might need financial help. Early in 1944 the Local Committee decided to replace " Limbourne " by means of an " Avenge the ' Limbourne ' " Week and eventually raised £143,000 to provide the Navy with a Frigate. This effort resulted in the adoption of H.M.S. " Evenlode " for which a Comforts Fund was also established. Happily, " Evenlode " came through the war unharmed. Among the many pleasant recollections for those who took part in these Weeks will be the visit to Dagenham of a party from H.M.S. " Evenlode " during " Avenge the ' Limbourne ' " Week. They spent a week here, touring factories and schools to the delight of both. Entertaining talks were given to the workers and school children proving, if proof were needed, that the Navy is not always the Silent Service.

After one old admiral had made his speech, the next speaker was a stoker. He explained that he was quite unused to public speaking and had no idea what to say. " But," he added, " what a smashing lot of girls there are in this factory ! " It was adequate for the occasion and did the cause a lot of good.

" Wings for Victory " Week in 1943 was devoted to the interests of the Royal Air Force. The Local Committee set out to raise £425,000 to provide five Bombers and forty-five Fighters. The successful accomplishment of this task was recognised by the presentation of a commemorative plaque which now hangs in the Civic Centre. The Borough will also receive the log-books of five aircraft, containing details of their war-time operations, which will find a place of honour in the Civic Centre.

For " Salute the Soldier " Week (1944) Dagenham's target was £450,000, the cost of equipping eight Paratroop battalions and two Medical Units and a third plaque bears witness to yet another successful achievement.

" Thanksgiving " Week (1945), the last of these events, produced the largest sum of money recorded by Dagenham in any week—£642,000. A specially bound book containing thanksgiving messages from Their Majesties the King and Queen, Princess Elizabeth, the Prime Minister and many other notable people, will be presented to the Borough.

These special Weeks were valuable both for the money they made available to the Treasury and for the excitement and incentive they gave to the vast army of voluntary workers in the National Savings Movement. They were undoubtedly responsible for much of the steady and substantial progress in ordinary week by week saving.

Dagenham has been in competition with its neighbours, Romford and Hornchurch, since 1942. A Shield, provided by the three Local Committees, is awarded each year to the town with the best percentage of group members in relation to its population. Hornchurch held this trophy until 1945, when it passed to Dagenham.

The following statistics show the extent of Dagenham's contribution to National Savings between 1st October, 1939 and 31st December, 1945 :—

Year ending 31st Mar.	Special Week	Money raised in special week	Money raised during the year
		£	£
1939–40*	——	—	102,000
1940–41	War Weapons Week . .	429,000	863,000
1941–42	Warships Week . .	491,000	1,086,000
1942–43	——	—	780,000
1943–44	Wings for Victory Week .	522,000	1,736,000
	Avenge the " Limbourne " Week . . .	143,000	
1944–45	Salute the Soldier Week .	631,000	1,883,000
1945–46†	Thanksgiving Week . .	642,000	1,111,000
			£7,561,000

* From 1st October, 1939.
† To 31st December, 1945.

War Charities

It is impossible to compute what sum of money was raised for War Charities in Dagenham. The list given here is those Charities sponsored by the Borough Council or raised under the patronage of the Mayor. But this is not half the story. The hundreds of small funds collected in streets, in public houses, in shops, in factories, and under a variety of private arrangements, yielded a sum which can only be guessed, but no more than that.

Roughly, £13,000 was raised by officially sponsored appeals but it would not be an unreasonable guess to multiply this sum by three times to get a fairer picture of local generosity.

Appeals for the Merchant Navy by three successive Mayors brought in the sum of nearly £5,000. That is a very handsome contribution from workers' pockets. Two naval ships were adopted, H.M.S. " Limbourne " (lost in action) and H.M.S. " Evenlode." Over £1,000 was raised for comforts for these two ships.

One note must be added concerning the charity first on the list. This was not raised in Dagenham. It was money raised by the Lord Mayor of London from England and all the world (*urbi et orbi* so to speak) for the immediate relief of air raid distress. We got exactly what we asked for and it came at once without formality—over £15,000 in cash and £700 in kind. Every other blitzed town or place had the same experience.

(*a*) LORD MAYOR OF LONDON AIR RAID DISTRESS FUND

	£	s.	d.
Total Cash Grants	15,343	11	9
Assistance in kind . . . . . Over	700	0	0

(*b*) APPEALS AND FLAG DAYS YEARS 1941 to 1946

1941–1942 (Alderman Clack—Mayor)

		£	s.	d.
9/ 6/42	Red Cross Flag Day . . .	150	13	2
16/ 6/42	Flag Day for Seamen . . .	43	2	2
9/42	Merchant Navy Week . . .	1,700	0	0

1942–1944 (Alderman Mrs. Evans—Mayor)

		£	s.	d.
—	H.M.S. " Limbourne " Comforts Fund	574	15	8
—	Y.M.C.A. War Service Fund .	132	17	0
1/12/42	Red Cross Prisoners of War Fund .	645	1	4
23/ 3/43	United Aid to China Fund . .	175	0	0
13/ 4/43	Flag Day for Seamen . . .	92	3	4
18/ 5/43	Lifeboat Day	74	8	1
5/43	Y.W.C.A. War-time Appeal . .	88	0	0
12/43	Merchant Navy Week . . .	2,300	0	0
8/ 6/43	Red Cross Flag Day . . .	307	2	7
28/ 8/43	Aid to Russia Flag Day . .	181	8	3
—	Dagenham Forces House, 1943–1944	919	6	10
—	Dagenham Forces House, 1944–1945	382	13	1
3/44	United Aid to China Flag Day .	189	0	0
4/44	Flag Day for Seamen . . .	45	16	1
5/44	Lifeboat Day	16	3	10
5/44	Essex County War Welfare Fund .	703	5	2
6/ 6/44	Red Cross Flag Day . . .	237	2	11
17/10/44	Aid to Russia Flag Day . .	121	13	10

1944-1945 (Alderman F. Brown—Mayor)

		£	s.	d.
—	H.M.S. "Evenlode" Comforts Fund	371	9	2
—	S.E.A.C.	185	17	0
6/ 1/45	Major Tasker Watkins, V.C. Fund .	65	0	0
10/ 4/45	Flag Day for Seamen . . .	185	11	11
5/ 6/45	Red Cross Flag Day . . .	118	4	2
45	Aid to Russia	69	14	4
45	United Aid to China Fund . .	71	14	4
5/45	Essex County War Welfare Fund .	74	8	5

1945-1946 (Alderman Thomas—Mayor)

		£	s.	d.
—	H.M.S. "Evenlode" Comforts Fund	61	7	10
9/ 4/46	Flag Day for Seamen . . .	75	8	4
3/46	Y.P.O.C.	55	11	6
4/ 5/46	Merchant Navy Week . . .	547	8	10

(c) EVACUEES

	£	s.	d.
Amount expended on evacuees from their Welfare Fund	1,259	14	8
Borough Clothing Fund	689	14	4

(d) DAGENHAM WING A.T.C. WELFARE FUND

		£	s.	d.
1/8/41—31/7/42	Coun. Thomas, Chairman .	426	13	10
1/8/42—31/7/43	Coun. Thomas, Chairman .	121	9	9
1/8/43—31/7/44	Coun. Thomas, Chairman .	230	13	2
1/8/44—31/7/45	Coun. Grindrod, Chairman .	133	13	5
1/8/45—31/3/46	Coun. Grindrod, Chairman .	129	6	5

CHAPTER TEN

THE HOME GUARD, THE A.T.C. AND OTHER PRE-SERVICE UNITS AND INVASION DEFENCE

THE first battalion (known as " K " 1st Battalion) of the Local Defence Volunteers was formed in May, 1940, directly after the first appeal was made. There was no lack of recruits, many of whom had served in the first Great War.

On the 12th September, 1940 the Battalion was transferred to the Essex Territorial Association, and renamed the 11th C.O.L. (Essex) Battalion H.G. On the 1st March, 1941, the Battalion was transferred back to London Control and was renamed the 11th C. O. L. (Dagenham) Battalion H.G., the title which it retained until the end.

After many temporary homes, Battalion Headquarters was eventually situated in the Halbutt Street T.A. Drill Hall, and finally transferred to the Drill Hall, Wood Lane, Dagenham.

The Battalion originally consisted of three groups, as follows :—

" A " Company. South Dagenham, commanded by Capt. S. A. Smith, M.C.

" B " Company. Central Dagenham and Becontree, commanded by Lieut. W. V. Powell, assisted by Sgt. L. Calvert, V.C., M.M.

" C " Company. Chadwell Heath, commanded by Capt. A. W. Farnam.

but very soon the many great industrial works in Dagenham responded nobly to the appeal to raise Works Defence Units in the area and Messrs. Briggs Bodies, Ltd., Messrs. Ford Motor Company Ltd., Messrs. Murex, Ltd., Messrs. May & Baker, Ltd., Messrs. Samuel Williams & Co. and Messrs. S. E. Norris, Ltd., all raised their own Works Unit and encouraged their employees to join the G.S. Companies.

Assistance was also rendered in many instances by the loan of accommodation and other amenities and the Sterling Engineering Company was particularly helpful to " B " Companies supplying Company Headquarters a miniature range and many of the personnel. For some time all the Works Units were embraced by the organisational description " D " Company, and later, on the formation of a G.S. " D " Company, they were named " E," " F," " G," " H " and " J " Companies. In October, 1941, however, the Battalion parted with most of the Works Companies when the Works Units of Fords, Briggs, Murex, Samuel Williams and other small contingents were transferred together with other small units outside the Dagenham area to form the 7th C.O.L. (Rippleside) Battalion H.G.

The first Commander was Lt.-Col. S. A. Smith, M.C., who retained the command until May, 1941, when he was appointed 2nd i/Command of " K " Zone Headquarters. He was subsequently appointed as Commander " K " Sector Headquarters, and held that appointment until his resignation on the 11th April, 1944 to take service as a Colonel in the Regular Forces. Lt.-Col. F. S. Thirsk, M.C., who had previously served as O.C. " B " Company and 2nd i/Command of the Battalion, was appointed to command the Battalion in May, 1941, and continued to do so until the stand down.

The Battalion, which up till then had been the strength of an ordinary British Infantry Brigade, now became a much more compact unit, with four G.S. Companies, " A," " B," " C " and " D," each with an average establishment of 350 with the addition of the highly efficient force of about 150 provided by Messrs. May & Baker, Ltd. On the 24th June, 1942, the Battalion was again reorganised operationally. " C " Company at Chadwell Heath was transferred to the 12th Battalion, and " A " Company of the 12th Battalion was transferred to this unit.

In the spring of 1942, the Government decided to utilise the Home Guard for Anti-Aircraft Batteries. At this stage in the war little surprise was expressed at the replacement of trained gunners by spare-time soldiers and they (the latter) took up their new responsibilities eagerly. More recruits were sought for. Nine hundred men were recruited in Dagenham for this work by Major H. Parrish (a descendant of men who farmed Dagenham lands for many years), but the number of Anti-Aircraft increased and further demands on the battalion seriously reduced its strength. In addition to this, there were constant losses caused by men joining the regular forces. Training and organisation were difficult in such circumstances. Demands on the Home Guard by the Anti-Aircraft command increased and the whole of " C " Company, who reached the necessary physical standard, were posted to heavy anti-aircraft batteries on 12th December, 1943. The rest of the Company went to the 7th County of London and the whole Company was lost to the Dagenham Battalion.

The approximate number of men who passed through the Battalion during the formation was 5,163 (five thousand one hundred and sixty-three) and at " Stand down " the strength of the Battalion was 93 officers and 1,505 other ranks. The fact that only 232 of these had served in the Battalion since its inception, shows the extraordinary changes which had taken place in the composition of the Battalion and the administrative work entailed.

The Home Guard were fortunately never called upon to guard the home except those who became Anti-aircraft gunners. They served the home, however, in many ways, particularly in assisting the Civil Defence Services in air raid incidents. This was particularly so during " V.1 " and " V.2 " raids, when assistance in first aid repair to houses was a practicable Home Guard service. The men were working full-time in addition to Home Guard duties and this fact is more than worthy of record. It was not an easy force to maintain in a disciplined fashion. Everybody worked and spare time was the only time for Home Guarding. They were not only drilled and trained but they became enthusiastic shots. In the sector competitions five times they were second and once first. Four times the Battalion despatch riders won the sector riders trials. They bought a Silver Band from their own funds assisted by local subscriptions. The battles and camps at Hainault Forest and Purfleet were thoroughly enjoyed and, finally, the following funds were raised by the Battalion :—

			£	s.	d.
Royal Fusiliers P.O.W. Fund	.	.	171	3	6
Essex Regiment P.O.W. Fund	.	.	25	0	0
Essex Forces Welfare Association	.	.	40	0	0
Various Children's Hospitals .	.	.	65	0	0

The invasion defence organisation was deeply concerned with the Home Guard although the organisation was on a civilian basis. Dagenham, within the London Invasion Area, was part of its extreme eastern perimeter of the area.

The organisation was designed to preserve civil administration should invasion take place. A consultative board was formed representing all aspects of local government—Borough Council, County Council, and statutory companies concerned with gas, electricity and water. Each branch of the Civil Defence Services was represented, and also were officials of the National Fire Service, Metropolitan Police, Ministry of Food and the Women's Voluntary Services. Representatives of military units and the Home Guard also formed part of the Board.

The work of the invasion defence organisation was to preserve the fabric of civilian life—to undertake all emergency services for public welfare—to ensure the sheltering and feeding of the homeless, evacuation of the population, preservation of essential services such as water, power, gas and drainage.

The Controller of Civil Defence Services acted as Invasion Officer and six invasion districts were marked out under an Invasion Defence Warden. Co-operation with military requirements was the first consideration and the organisation undertook to keep all important roads free from debris and repaired after air raids.

Fire-fighting and the whole range of Civil Defence Services were to be devoted to aiding military movements, in the first place, and in providing every possible assistance for civilians, in the second. The plan and organisation set up for anti-invasion work was a very detailed and elaborate one. It covered every aspect of civilian life—every necessity was accounted for, and had invasion reached this area, this organisation would have been ready to co-operate with military plans and provided the necessities of life for the civilian population.

A.T.C.

The young boys in Air Force uniform are still to be seen, although in smaller numbers. During the war they made a formidable pre-service force, outstripping in numbers any other youth organisation.

The Air Training Corps was designed as a pre-service unit for young men. The Corps aimed at preparing youths for the Air Force. It was started at the beginning of 1941, and in the February of that year, the Dagenham Wing was formed. Squadron No. 227, the official title of the first unit, numbered two hundred cadets, with their four Flight Officers, Wills, Jarratt, Reece and Brown, and with Warrant Officer Earl. The last-named trained the Corps into a notable position in amateur boxing.

The Corps made the first public appearance on 16th February, 1941, with a March Past at the Civic Centre. The Salute was taken by the Mayor, Alderman Clack, and it was probably the first (or one of the first) occasions that a Mayor of Dagenham received such a military honour.

Recruitment was astonishingly rapid. Two further squadrons, numbers 1390 and 2048, were formed with Flight-Lieuts. Jarratt and Brown as officers. A Wing Commanding Officer was appointed (Flight-Lieut. Hamm) at this stage.

The Corps went into serious training. Classes in navigation, mathematics, etc., were organised and practical air training was provided at Hornchurch Aerodrome. It was, without question, the most successful of all pre-service units. Numbers are astonishing. Over six hundred Dagenham Air Training Cadets went into the Air Force. The significance of this fact can be measured by the part that air power played in the final victory. Recruitment was voluntary in the usual English manner.

The war record of the Dagenham Wing was honourable. The distinctions included two Distinguished Flying Medals, three Distinguished Flying Crosses, and eight cadets achieved commissioned rank, one becoming a Squadron Leader. All of these boys were products of the County Council schools and possessed no " advantages." There were many who did not return—theirs is the greatest honour.

As an aid to Welfare Funds for the A.T.C., a film entitled " Sons of the Air " was sponsored by official quarters. The Dagenham Wing figured prominently in it, not unnaturally, as the producer was their own Commanding Officer, Flight-Lieut. Edward Jarratt.

Trained by Warrant Officer Earl, the Wing won the A.T.C. All-England Boxing Championship held at the Albert Hall. It was the first championship of its kind and this success gave the most profound satisfaction to Dagenham people.

When Air Marshal Sir Leslie Gossage, Chief A.T.C. Commandant, paid a personal visit here, it was felt that it was very well deserved.

The A.T.C. did not finish with the war, it still goes on doing the same work.

Other pre-service units, such as the Navy Cadets and the Army Cadet Corps (Dagenham Unit) were busy on a smaller scale with the training of young men.

CHAPTER ELEVEN

THE WORKERS' SHARE:
INDUSTRIAL PRODUCTION

COMMENT and explanation on these figures of industrial production are superfluous. The men and women who did this work under skies that were at times in the possession of the enemy, were fighting their own war on a strange battlefield.

There is no Borough in England of a comparable size that can match such an output, and these are only the bulk figures. Many little workshops (and large ones) did countless small jobs.

FORD MOTOR COMPANY LIMITED

V8 Engines	268,788
Tracked vehicles	13,942
Wheeled vehicles	182,511
Tractors	120,281
Units of electricity	810,094,794

BRIGGS MOTOR BODIES LIMITED

Motor and armoured vehicles	278,000
Store ammunition boxes	8,000,000
Jerricans (petrol)	20,000,000
Steel helmets	11,000,000
Aircraft components	2,600,000
Rocket shells, bombs and components	2,500,000
Mines, sinkers and floats	150,000

MAY & BAKER LIMITED

Cycloral sodium ampoules for Russia and Allies (anesthesia)	5,000,000
Quinacine (Nepacine) Anti-Malaria tablets	550,000,000
M. and B. 693 (Dagan) tablets and other sulpha drugs	700,000,000
Menthol bromide (every plane carries fire extinguishers containing this)	

KELSEY HAYES WHEEL CO., LTD.
  Wheels 2,100,000

SOUTHERN UNITED TELEPHONES, LTD.
  Yards of telephone lines . . 4,500,000,000

STERLING ENGINEERING CO., LTD.
  Lanchester sub-machine guns and magazines
  Wellington bomb release gear
  " Airborne " electric motors and hydraulic controls
  Admiralty radar equipment

Messrs. WILLIAMS, Dagenham Dock
  Bulk handling

SPRINGCOT, LIMITED
  Air frames 1,154
  Parachutes 730,000
  Sleeping bags for paratroops . . . 185,000
  Gun slings 720,000
  Cotton felt . . . . . 4,500 tons
  Palliasses 750,000

PRITCHETT & GOLD LIMITED
  Power batteries 4,850,000

W. J. BARTON LIMITED
  Loaves 50,000,000

W. J. REYNOLDS LIMITED
  Equipped vehicles 8,000
  Handling war material . . . 10,000 tons

J. CROLLIE (LUBRICATION) LIMITED
  Air sea rescue equipment

A. W. SMITH & CO., LTD. (BOLENIUM)
  Overalls for the Services . . . 1,500,000

LAKESIDE IRONWORKS LIMITED
  Hot water cylinders, camp sinks and cisterns 31,000

Prepared and compiled by John O'Leary, Borough Librarian, in collaboration with Dr. C. Herington, H. O. Bigg, F. C. Stickland and P. T. Frost, and published by the Dagenham Borough Council in the month of May, 1947.

INDEX

The Drayton Press, East Ham, E.6

The Archives & Local Studies Centre at Valence House Museum in the London Borough of Barking & Dagenham is the source and inspiration for many local heritage projects. When volunteers working there wish to develop and expand topics of significant local historical interest they are encouraged with the generous support of the professional staff.

This publication is a scanned reproduction of the book originally published in 1947. Barking and Dagenham currently has two books of remembrance which list all those who died during World War Two, however little has been done to keep our official memorials up to date since 1945. We would like to rectify this by producing a third book with the names of all the men and women from Barking and Dagenham who have died on active service, serving their country, from World War Two onwards.

All money raised from this publication will go to this project.

Lightning Source UK Ltd.
Milton Keynes UK
UKHW021023271220
375899UK00009B/1073